ISBN # 0-9746114-4-1
PUBLISHED BY TWO DOWN PRESS INC.
PRINTED IN THE USA

The 21st. Century Golf Swing

By *Dan Shauger*
Author of
"How to Kill the Ball"

THE FORMULA FOR POWER AND ACCURACY SERIES

THE "APERFECTSWING" METHOD

Introduction

August 22, 2006

Like so many other golfers, I came to Dan hoping to find the secret of distance. What I learned was a lot more than that. I gained a greater understanding of the golf swing, a new putting style and much more accuracy in ball striking. All of this translates to an enormous increase in my enjoyment and satisfaction on the golf course.

I met Dan while researching my book In Search of the Greatest Golf Swing; Chasing the Legend of Mike Austin. I was interesting in hearing the Mike Austin swing described by a different, more patient teacher. While I progressed as a student, Dan improved even more as a teacher and writer. Already a good teacher, Dan has grown enormously and become a real authority on the golf swing while improving the ability of many beginning, intermediate and expert players.

What you hold in your hands represents years of work and a lifetime of thought. It is also the result of the hours Dan spent teaching and watching students struggling to learn golf. While hands-on teaching is the best way to learn golf I believe this book is the next best thing. You can study the concepts in this book at your leisure, absorb them fully and refer to them later to refresh your memory.

But be prepared, this swing is different than what is normally taught by the golfing establishment. While it doesn't look very different, a number of principles are nearly the opposite of what is commonly taught.

Naturally, you may be wondering what kind of results I got using the golf swing taught in this book. I saw immediate progress and greater accuracy. There were times, though, that I got off track and was frustrated. However, I sensed that I was on the right course and kept working with Dan. I also read many drafts of this book. My distance went from occasionally hitting 210-yard drives to seeing several 270-yard drives in the same round of golf. Last March, in Denver, Colorado, I hit a drive 336 yards. It was on a soft, level fairway with a slight wind behind me.

Since it is easier to brag about someone else than myself, I have decided to include a quick word about one of Dan's other students. Gary Sanati began taking lessons from Dan only a little over a year ago. I've played many rounds with Gary where he has hit the ball way over 300 yards. I saw him hit it 340 yards into the wind. It's funny to begin the round of golf getting matched up with a two-some of big lugs. They act unimpressed by Gary, who is probably only five feet, ten inches tall. Unimpressed, that is, until he hits his driver. Then they can't figure out how he hits the ball so far. One, a six footer, with a powerful swing, found Gary was hitting the ball 40 yards past him. His manner became subservient in the presence of the alpha male.

Recently, my thirst for distance has given way to a desire for greater accuracy (in fact, the longer you are the more accuracy is required). I've refocused on Dan's teaching from a different point of view. While long drives will make you the envy of your golf buddies, serious golfers will use accurate ball striking to win tournaments and lower their handicaps.

Now you, like Dan's other students, can look forward to becoming the golfer you always dreamed of being. See you on the tee box!

Philip Reed

The Champions

At this writing your author has had the pleasure to work with 3 long drive competitors, since then each of them has had success entering and winning major long driving contests nationwide. John Marshall 2005 and 2006 ALDA Super Senior National Champion and 2006 Remax Worlds Long Driving Championship finalist. Jim Liska first runner up to Marshall in the 2006 ALDA Nationals who is also a 2005-2006 ReMax Worlds Long Driving Championship finalist in the Super Seniors division. The third is 28 year old Jaacob Bowden 2003 Pinnacle Distance Challenge Champion (St. Louis). Marshall and Liska had taken a combined total of 5 hours instruction in this method. Jaacob went from a 14 handicap player who's longest drive was 280 and uncontrolled to a professional golfer in 4 months. He won his championship with a drive of 381 yards, on level ground with a cross wind, 2 months after turning pro.

They attained this success by not only increasing the distance they hit the ball, but more importantly by gaining the accuracy needed to be able to hit the ball into the grid. In long drive competitions it doesn't mean a thing to hit the ball a mile if it did not go where you are aiming it. The same is true for playing the game of golf, gaining yardage is good, but if it costs you accuracy it is not. It may even be a lot worse. The grid width in long driving competitions is generally 40 yards, although some competitions may allow a 50 yard grid. This may sound large, but when the ball is flying well over 300 yards (330 or more is very common on the fly for these players) the area gets considerably tighter. The farther you hit the ball, the more off line the ball ends up should you not hit it on line, or if it has any unintended curvature. The street in front of your house is probably 50 feet wide, that is 1/3 of 50 yards. If you simply look 300 or more yards down your street you can see how narrow it appears, at that distance your 50 foot street looks little bigger than a sidewalk, in long drive competitions and especially under pressure 40 to 50 yards looks very small indeed.

The swing I will be describing in these pages will give you more yardage, in some cases a lot more. More importantly it will give you precision golf shots that will fly straight with little or no unwanted curvature (unless you want the ball to curve).

Most players that I work with in person immediately gain 20 or 30 yards with the pitching wedge, we can calculate how much gain that would be on a driver by thinking in percentages. If the player started with 100 yards with his wedge but increased it to 120 yards he would have gained 20%. When he hits his driver equally well he would gain 20% additional distance with that club. If he could hit his driver 230 yards before he learned this method, he would gain 46 yards for a total of 276 yards. Your distance gains should be similar, but results vary. Your accuracy will definitely improve. The longest drive is the one closest to the hole not the one farthest from the tee.

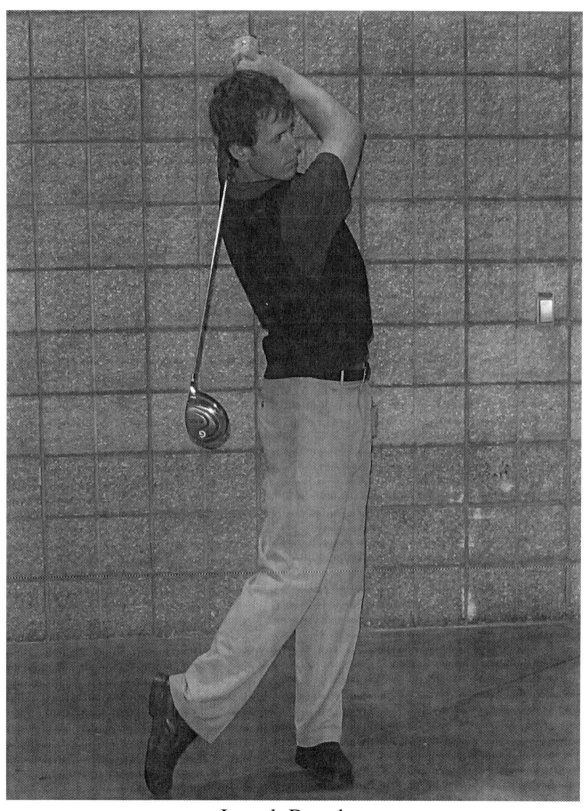

Jaacob Bowden
Pinnacle Distance Challenge Champion
St. Louis MO 2003

Foreword By Jaacob Bowden

I first met Dan Shauger on a cold and extremely windy day in January of 2003 on the driving range of Lost Canyons Golf Club in Simi Valley, California.

The winds were gusting so furiously that it was nearly impossible to keep our bags from blowing over, our hats on our heads and our balance. Dan was hitting balls behind me, and as I took a back swing to hit the ball an especially hard gust blew me backwards nearly onto him. I may well have bumped into him, were it not for the same gust of wind blowing him backwards as well.

We chuckled over our dedication to practicing in such adverse conditions and we began talking about our respective backgrounds. Dan was soon to turn 63, was retired from a career in the movie industry, and had been teaching golf in the Los Angeles area for the last seven years. He was at Lost Canyons that day because he was considering membership. I had turned 27 earlier in the month, and had recently resigned from a computer engineering job that I had unhappily held in Kansas City and St. Louis for the last four and one half years. I had packed all of my belongings, left my home, friends and family and moved to California to pursue my dream of being a professional golfer on the PGA tour.

At the time I was a 14 handicap and was rather unspectacular at golf; however, both through my own study and also from two or three lessons from a PGA teaching professional, I had become fairly familiar with the fundamentals that were currently being taught by the golf world. I was set on using my time and my $40,000 in savings from my old job to become good enough to turn pro by the end of the year. It was an outrageous goal, but I was young, adventurous and willing to make whatever sacrifice or risk necessary to achieve my goal.

They say that when the student is ready, the master will appear. In our case, I think it could also be said that when the master is ready the student will appear. I believe that Dan and I met for a reason. We needed one another to help fulfill each others' goals. Dan knew more about the golf swing than anyone I had ever met. He had studied closely under the legendary Mike Austin who had given Dan an understanding of a different way of swinging the golf club. Dan told me of Mike's 515 yard drive hit with the unique swing he developed and how he trained Dan to be a teaching professional. The story intrigued me and I decided to learn the swing from Dan if I could.

I was looking for an edge, and since I was financially limited, I needed someone like Dan to take me under his wing. The fundamentals that Dan professed were out of the ordinary, yet at the same time his ideas made sense. He was looking for a young, dedicated protégé who would listen and be open to what he had to say. He needed someone who would pick up on his teachings and then go out and prove that his revolutionary teachings worked by having his student win at the highest levels of golf. That was how the relationship began. Dan and I worked together fairly heavily for four or five days each week in February and March, braving cold days and fierce winds. At first my drives were all over the place and each day I had no idea what was in store for me.

By April I was getting so long and straight that someone suggested entering a long drive contest. I entered my first competition in May 2003 in Phoenix, AZ.. I took 8th place out of over 120 competitors with a 343 yard drive. In my 5th event I beat out over 150 competitors by hitting one 381 yards to win the Pinnacle Distance Challenge in St. Louis! Over the rest of the 2003 season, I realized my dream of becoming a professional golfer, entered approximately 15-18 long drive championships, averaged 336.8 yards per drive, never once completely missed the grid, got to the District Finals of the ReMax World Long Drive Championships, increased my clubhead speed to 144 mph, hit one of my drives 400 yards in a mini tour event with a (45 inch driver), lowered my best 18 hole score from 78 to 69, and eliminated all of the back and knee pain I was having using the fundamentals commonly taught in golf today.

Without Dan's knowledge and support, I never would have come close to accomplishing what I did in 2003. And it is this knowledge and support that I hope will take me to the top of the golf world. There truly is a golf swing that is long, straight and easy on the body. Dan knows how to teach it. Many of the concepts he will introduce to you will seem to be the reverse of what is taught in to days market, but trust them and learn with an open mind. By doing so you will soon have an effortless-looking, beautiful, and powerful golf swing that I use to hit those long and straight, drives that most people only dream about.

Thank you Dan, for everything that you have done for me. You are without a doubt the number one teacher in the game of golf, and what you have to offer will revolutionize the way the game is played.

Jaacob Bowden
Winner of the Pinnacle Distance Challenge, St. Louis MO. 2003

How This Book Came To Be

This book was written in response to the overwhelming number of inquiries about how to learn more about this wonderful swing. It is based on my own thinking, even though the building blocks for this knowledge were laid by some of golfs heavyweights. By taking some of what I learned from a lifetimes pursuit of golf knowledge studying books, tapes DVDs and personal lessons, and adding it to my own original thoughts and concepts this method was born. It is unlike the teachings of anyone that I learned from, this teaching method is uniquely mine. It was not written with rank beginners in mind, but can be useful to anyone who picks up well from the printed page.

It is a natural follow up to my original book "How to Kill the Ball"/ The Formula For Power And Accuracy. If you have not read it you should, it gives the fundamentals for this swing, without the knowledge contained there this book will be more difficult to learn from. This basic knowledge, plus my advancements in the concepts of the circular club rotation, when put together create the perfect golf swing. The logic applied to the creation of this perfect golf swing is laid out in these pages in a way that allows the reader to follow the thinking in a simple progression, and thus see a complex collection of motions as a one piece unit.

Those who have read the original book will find some pages to be quite similar to pages in that book. Please forgive me for plagiarizing myself, but since I could not think of a better way to say those things I thought it best to just repeat them. Close attention should be paid though since every page has been revised.

To those who urged me to write more, I can only say thank you, this book is a tribute to you for your further quest for knowledge. The writing of it has also expanded my golf arsenal of teaching terms, it has given me many new ways to express myself as I teach.

Sometimes simply writing things on paper seems to connect you to the knowledge of the universe. I feel blessed to be the conduit that brings it to you. I hope that you, the reader, and everyone else who reads this material enjoys the same level of improvement that my students who have taken personal lessons have.

For those who wish to see the swing in action and further visual teachings by me the DVDs available on the web site www.aperfectswing.com should be consulted. They are each unique and the information is presented in a way that allows the knowledge contained in them to be added together. Lessons are available from Dan in California, as well as a staff here in the USA and around the world.

This book details subtle differences between the Long Driving contest type golf swing I wrote about in How to Kill the Ball and a less violent, more controlled action for playing golf for score. It is a swing that still produces excellent power, giving up only a little of the distance possible when swinging all out.

The giving up of a small amount of potential distance is a small price to pay for the increase in accuracy that you will gain. My long drive champions use this method to get a good ball into the grid before going for the fences, often that shot is good enough to win.

The 21st Century Golf Swing has not been written as a primer for beginners, and does not deal much with the fundamentals of the golf swing. For a complete understanding of the grip, stance, posture and balance the other book should be consulted. If you are already a somewhat accomplished golfer, you can modify your basic swing motions quickly by incorporating the concept of the swing and the hand release as it is detailed here. However to truly "get it" you should consider undertaking the learning of this as a complete beginner. The fundamentals of this swing create slightly different body angles and the way that the body produces power from those angles is probably much different from the way that you now do it. These elements of the golf swing together with the understanding of the design of the golf club itself and how that design influences every action of the swing are discussed in great depth there. For perfection the fundamental elements learned in the other book must be used since they provide the most accurate and perfect way to hold the club and attain a stance that will function with complete precision.

This swing although slightly less powerful than the HTKTB swing still generates immense controlled power and, once the mind grasps its concept, learning it is not exceptionally difficult to do. The total concept of the twirling clubhead in the conical action is something I envisioned based on some clues I got as to its possibilities from the late Mike Austin, although he never used it himself. I also will outline in this book, one of the secrets that I think went to the grave with the late, great Ben Hogan.

For those who have not studied the original book the concept of what we are doing will surprise you. It is radically different from what you have been doing, and will require some practice to both groove the new motions and eliminate or modify the old. The effort to learn this swing, will be paid back to you by the lesser amount of effort swinging the club and playing golf will be for you. I and many others feel that this is truly the golf swing of the future and perhaps will someday be the way that it is universally taught.

Dedications

I dedicate this book to my lady, Elaine, for all the loving support she has given me through the ordeal of giving birth to this book. Having her in my life is what makes it worth living. She has the heart of a saint, and physical beauty too.

This book like my others would never have come to pass without much help from many people that I am privileged to call my friends. Here is a short list.

First I must thank my good friend Orlando De Guevara for getting me going with the computer, as I have said before without his help this would have been scribbled on a paper bag, in pencil. With my handwriting it would have taken a team of a few dozen Egyptologists decades to decipher it.

Thanks goes out to Phil Reed for his editorial assistance, praise and guidance. I know that I will never attain his prowess as a writer, but his help improves me daily. Thanks also to Professor Emeritus Arthur DeVany for his early proof reading of my words, and spurring me to make the book better.

Thanks also to my Champions, John Marshall, Jim Liska and Jaacob Bowden both for being Champions and also for posing for the pictures in the book. May they continue with their success, with their help we can pass this information on through their teachings. They all have become very fine instructors with much swing knowledge and the skills to demonstrate it.

Thanks to Rocky Kinsey for self teaching himself, from the book and DVDs with just a small amount of guidance from me, to the level of instructor. He and many others like him worldwide have proven that what I write and the DVDs I make can help people teach themselves.

Thanks to William Wetere for taking the aperfectswing method to New Zealand, he is another instructor of this wonderful swing. I wish him much success as well.

Thanks also to my students, who also modeled for photos, John Marshall, Jim Liska, Jaacob Bowden, Gary Sanati, and his son G.J. Sanati both of whom have made big gains both as ball strikers and as players. As has Mike Foster who shows that tall players can do this too.

I must also thank my many students worldwide who by buying my books and DVDs, and taking lessons from me have financed me during the time it has taken to conceive and write this. I hope that I have not tried your collective patience, too badly, and that the info in this book makes the wait worth while.

TABLE OF CONTENTS

How It Works
The Concept

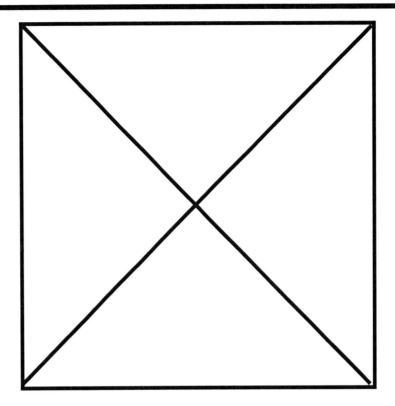

A pyramid, seen from directly above, looks very different from the way it looks when you are standing at ground level the same distance away. If the above sketch was the only view you had of it you might be surprised at what the other view below shows.

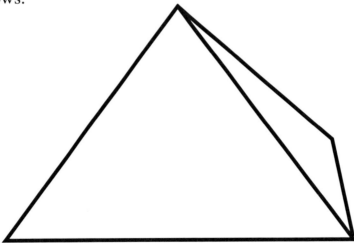

That square with the big X in it suddenly takes on a whole new shape. When we see it from another angle, what we thought we saw may not actually be what we now see. We could say we changed our point of view, here we will get a new point of view of the golf swing. When you change how you see it, you will change how you do it. Changing your concept will give you;
                    "The Swing of the Future".

Concept

Our concept of, what it takes to do whatever it is we want to do, is what governs how we do it. A perfect example of this is the actions necessary to steer a bicycle or a motorcycle, compared to the same actions done on a tricycle.

One reason that children have a hard time learning to ride a bicycle is that they have started out learning how to ride something else, either a tricycle or a bicycle with training wheels. On both of those devices to turn left you turn the bars to the left, and a left turn is what you get.

A bicycle however has different dynamics, and even if you have learned how to ride one, you probably do not know exactly how a bicycle turns. You can do it because you have done it, sort of, but when you know how it turns you can do it much more efficiently.

To turn a bicycle or a motorcycle you actually need to turn the bars the opposite way. Here is why; by moving the bars a little in the opposite direction we actually cause the bike to fall over, and create a lean angle in the direction we want to turn. Try this, ride a 2 wheeler at 10 to 15 mph in a parking lot or schoolyard, gently push the left bar forward a tiny bit as if you were turning right, sit upright and don't lean. The bike will quickly lean left, release the pressure and the bike turns in the arc you have created. If you keep pushing on it the lean angle will increase until you fall off. Please don't fall off. This is how a bike turns, and when you learn how it works riding one becomes much easier. From that moment on you will never go back to the old way of riding, because your new concept works better. The new concept then directs your actions and before long you do it without thinking. Your concept has solidified into actions. The reverse rotation of the winding and unwinding forearms seems at first to be as wrong as turning a bikes bars right to go left. Once felt there will be no doubt as to how well it works.

The same thing happens every time we make a concept change, if we do it the new way and it works better we abandon the old way of thinking and doing. In other words to change how we do something requires a different way of looking at it, and "seeing" it; this is a concept change.

The most important thing you will learn from this book is how to see your golf swing, in your minds eye, as you have never seen it before. When you change the concept, of how you do what you do, you will step off in an entirely different direction. A change like this requires a little time to "take", be patient with your self the results are worth it.

An Apple And An Orange, Similar But Very Different

Both are round fruits and good for you, but the resemblance ends there.
So it is with this golf swing, it resembles other methods but is quite different.

A DIFFERENT WAY TO SWING THE CLUB

The swing that you will be learning here is quite different from the standard golf swing. If you have been shown a difficult way of doing a complex task you should not be surprised if you have had a difficult time doing that task. Modern golf instruction is a collection of axioms passed down, as this is the way you do it, with very little outside the box thinking. Nearly all instruction uses the same basic concept of how to do it. Not in this book, here you will find a swing like no other, but so logical in its design as to be quickly understood as better.

This book is about hitting the ball long and straight, but within these pages and the videos that work with it you will also learn the secrets of trajectory and curvature control. This is a sequel to "How to Kill the Ball" / The Formula for Power and Accuracy, It is the second book of the series, if I discover unanswered questions from the feed back of this book I may write another. If you have not read it you should because it gives much basic information not covered here.

As of this writing 5 DVDs are available to assist your learning, I will soon produce several more, they together with the books will give you a masters degree in your understanding of this wonderful swing and the game we all love.

Hitting Versus Swinging

If we analyze the way that the ball can be struck we can come up with at least 2 very different types of actions, should the act of making a golf shot be a swing? Or should it be a hit?

In a swinging type action the club is pulled and swings out toward the ground when the arc reaches the point where gravity extends the lever (the golf club). This happens when the club approaches the bottom of the swing.

In the hit style of swing, the right arm slams the club into the back of the ball. Great golf can be played with either type of action and both are widely used. This swing uses both, combined with a dynamic use of the body weight. Due to this, the 21st Century golf swing has extra power and actually takes less effort. This swing also controls the plane and angle of attack in an entirely different way as a unique hand and arm action keeps the clubface square yet at the same time gives it extra speed.

The exact description of how this swing works is, the legs and feet shift the weight and turn the body around a fixed point. This action rotates the triangle of the shoulders and the arms. By flexing and extending the elbows and using the natural sliding actions of the shoulder blades the triangle moves the clubhead an additional 180 or more degrees farther than the body turns. The triangle by collapsing and extending its sides adds the extension power of the right arm to the movement of the hands as the hands create additional clubhead speed by twirling the club, which swings freely from the wrists and hits the ball.

In order to do these actions we must use the spine as both an axle and a lever. We also need to change our concept from hitting or swinging to doing both.

The more complete the picture of the action is to the minds eye (the internal vision of what we are doing) the more likely the swing is to perform perfectly.

Every action of the body throughout our daily lives is preceded by a mental picture of what you want to do and of your body doing it. Program the body for success with a pure concept and a clear mental picture of what you want to accomplish and you are half way there. The other half of the way will be gotten through preparation, by making enough correct swings to make the actions of the body a matter of feel, so that the conscious mind can get out of the way of the subconscious mind and allow the picture to complete itself.

THE FORMULA FOR POWER AND ACCURACY

Swing Overview

Here is a list of some of the features of this swing as opposed to the common swing:

•The shift of the weight will provide much of the power, rather than the turn of the torso.

•The turn will come later and will be done with a running action of the feet and legs.

•The head will remain still as the hips move up and down as well as laterally, rather than the head moving sideways as the entire spine moves forward and around.

•The ball will be struck more off the side of the body, rather than in front of the body.

•The torque created by the wind up of the torso in the back swing will not be released until very late in the down swing, thus using maximum leg action. Rather than an un-wind of the trunk muscles, which utilizes much less leg action, losing power.

•There will be no attempt to rotate the chest, the turn instead will be a product of the ac-tions of the feet and knees, which shift and rotate the hips, rather than an effort of chest and shoulder rotation. The strain on the spine will be greatly reduced as will injuries.

•The left arm will remain pressed to the chest throughout the down swing and will not leave the chest until after the ball is struck. Done this way it is driven first by the shift of weight, and later by the rotation of the spine. Rather than swinging from the shoulder socket, it will rotate with the spine just as a spoke would rotate with its axle.

•The right arm will throw the clubhead through the ball in a circular twirling motion around the left forearm and wrist. Like a ball swings around a maypole.

•The right arm accelerates the clubhead, starting from the top, rather than attempting to hold an angle for a "late" release.

•The forearms will not roll over as the club passes through impact, as is commonly done. Due to this the right hand will pass between the left hand and the ball, not roll over it.

•The right heel will lift early in the down swing and will be off the ground and rotating up on to the toe at impact, rather than remaining planted, and then rising after impact.

•The clubface will rotate around the shaft much less and be square much longer through the hitting area, rather than coming hosel first, and rolling suddenly to square the clubface.

•The entire swinging action of the club will feel to be conical, rather than round. The clubhead, as it swings in a conical manner, will not change planes during the swing.

•The ball will fly higher and with no curvature, rather than needing either a draw or a fade for control, unless these shot types are desired and intentionally caused.

•Trajectory control will be greatly simplified, and ball position is much less of an issue.

On the following pages each of these differences will be illustrated, and explained.

Out Over And Around

The common release requires a roll over of the arms to square up the blade. The clubface motion can be described as coming hosel first, then having the toe of the club roll out, over and around the shaft. This hopefully squares the club at impact. The continued roll after the hit then finds the toe of the club leading. This is a very similar action to the way one would swing a baseball bat. This type motion is fine for baseball since the bat is round and does not require getting a flat side positioned correctly at impact. The golf club creates quite a different situation, we must get the blade aligned properly or we get a shot that is either shanked, not struck solidly or if close to but not quite square, has unexpected curvature. Curvature is useful if planned for, but potentially a disaster if not.

The release action of the club learned here eliminates the opening and closing of the blade through the hit. This release of the clubhead can be described as down, under and up, with the clubface approaching the ball square but slightly de-lofted and passing through normal loft to slightly increased loft through the hit.

Swinging the club in this manner, will give both an increase in distance and more accurate direction control, as well as a much better ability to get the ball up out of the rough. Due to the unique way that the club swings from the wrists, your shots will fly higher allowing for quicker stopping on the green and giving you the additional ability of using a lower lofted driver which creates less back spin for longer drives. The difference in control and the solidity of contact should be felt immediately.

The 21st. Century release requires a slightly different hand and forearm position at the top of the back swing to function to its maximum. The reasons for this will soon be abundantly clear. The photos on the next 2 pages will help you see the release differently.

This swing just as any swing requires proper execution, if the components are not done in the prescribed manner the action will be flawed. If you make the error of getting the clubface positioned in the standard manner and then make the 21st Century body, arm and hand motions you will hit a weak shot high, right and slicing. That said, from this back swing position the standard release motions cause the clubface to quickly turn over and shut down producing a duck hook.

Your history must be re-written and the longer that you have made an action the more important the grooving of a new motion is, this has been done in as little as 30 days.
To see how a good swing looks, see pages 34-35. View it often.

The Standard Release Of The Club

In the common golf swing, the club is cocked vertically, and rolled open, in an effort to keep it in line with the rotated left arm. When rolled open it also opens the clubface. Since the clubface is open it returns to the ball hosel first, from there the only way to hit a solid square shot is to roll it back to square and continue rolling it until the club is traveling toe first up to the finish. This type release requires the forearms to roll over and, hopefully, time the turn of the clubface back to square.

This rolling action requires a vertical wrist cock, thus the toe of the club rises relative to the hands. Returning to the ball the release uses a sort of chopping down, axe type hit. This must be accompanied with the forearm rolling over action through the ball and then an un-chopping action as the club comes back up. The motion of the clubhead is best described as an out, over and around type motion.

For solid impact the right arm must perfectly time the roll over the left, therein lies the potential error. The ball must be placed in a precise location so that the club strikes the ball at the brief instant that it is properly aligned. Any other placement of the ball makes it very hard to hit due to the small time the blade is square.

Un-cocking The Wrists Down Combined With The Forearm Roll

The standard arm release actions seen in the photos above roll the clubhead and clubface around the shaft, as the wrists un-cock the hands vertically as if chopping wood. The timing of this chop and roll must be perfect to produce an accurate golf shot. Releasing this way the clubhead always remains in line with the left arm, it does not pass the point of the triangle, instead it re-cocks up.

The Common Golf Swing

In these photos the hand actions of the common (roller type) of arm action can be seen.

Imagine that Gary is standing in a room the size of the mat, with 4 walls and a ceiling and that the mat is the floor. As he swings back using the common concept you can see the hand has rotated open and is now facing the wall in front of him. Continuing up he arrives at the top with his palm facing halfway between the ceiling and the wall in front of him. Starting down his right hand comes down in a karate chop type of action, it arrives at hip high or a little below with the palm still facing the wall in front of him. From the position in the photo (below left) he will have to roll the forearm over to square the blade.

The photos above and below show how that must be done, it should kind of remind you of the spoon sending the ice cream who knows where in HTKTB. This type action requires excellent timing, and requires practice to keep it sharp.

Baseball Type Swing

Here again we see the classic roll the club open and then closed action of the common golf swing. Great for baseball, not so good for golf. In this type of action the face of the club is revolving around the shaft, and the forearms must roll over during the hitting and wrist un-cock sequence. The basic concept is of using the left arm and club as a flail, with the club remaining in line with the left arm throughout the motion. This action does not advance the shaft or blade past the center of the triangle. The club thus travels through impact in a straight line with the left arm which is also rolling. The clubhead does not advance instead it re-cocks up. Doing this does not take advantage of ones ability to use the full set of forearm muscles to add power. Less muscles used = less power. More effort is then needed to hit the same distance or perhaps less distance. Hitting with more effort further increases the possibility of a miss timed hit. Hitting with ease to produce good power is "The Formula For Power And Accuracy".

Floor To Ceiling Versus Wall To Wall

Here we show a major difference in the way this swing works versus the common roll over arm actions. The photos will show this graphically.

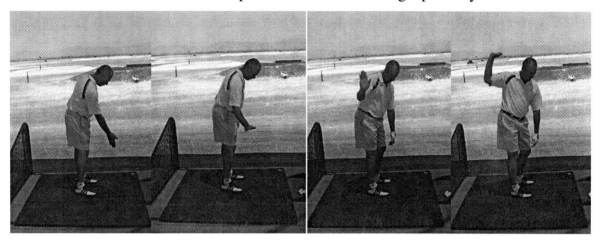

Here he is again in the same room, the right hand is facing the far wall and the target. In our swing this is the sequence of our right hand directions. Starting from the top left photo the palm is facing the far wall or target ward, starting back it first faces the floor, then the near wall, then the ceiling. Swinging down; the ceiling, near wall, floor, far wall, ceiling, near wall and finally the floor. The hands in this swing work floor to ceiling to floor, not wall to wall.

The down under and up action is readily apparent when seen this way, contrast this action with the out over and around movements of the common golf swing on the facing page and you will quickly understand just how much better this type swing action is. Once learned it requires little up keep.

THE FORMULA FOR POWER AND ACCURACY

The 21st Century Release
The photos and captions will save a lot of text. We describe our release as "Down, Under and Up".

Here Gary Sanati shows the release.

In these 2 photos the body actions have been reduced to show only the arm and club motions, later photos will clarify the body actions through impact. As the club swings through the left wrist and elbow are straight until impact and then shortly thereafter the left wrist flexes as does the left elbow and shoulder joints. As the clubhead swings through the left arm relaxes and simply folds into the arc of the extending right arm. These arm and wrist actions cause the clubhead to swing like a pendulum beneath the triangle, allowing a total release of energy into the ball, with a straight and very high (if we choose) ball flight. This release action works the clubface from closed to open rather than from open to closed. The chapter on the hand and wrist actions contains more photos and descriptions.

When the club releases this way, the right hand can toss the clubhead past the point of the triangle. The right hand adds speed and thus power to the hit and at the same time gives accurate direction by keeping the clubface square to the hit throughout the release sequence. This right hand release is what sends the ball high and straight, it allows a full hard hit without any fear of an unwanted hook. It also eliminates the slice by removing the roll that if not perfectly timed may give a miss-aligned clubface. In this or any other type swing you <u>must</u> hit through the ball, not at the ball, the left wrist <u>must</u> hinge and the right hand <u>must</u> hit through. Using this swing action those things will happen naturally. Our wrists as they release hinge sideways and thus freely swing the club.

Using this release produces a high ball flight. Because the clubface is square, and moving straight down the flight path, we gain a large area in which to place the ball for control of its flight. Placing the ball back produces a lower flight. Moving it forward produces a higher flight.

The ball flies straight regardless of whether its flight is high or low.

The Split Hand Drill

Here John Marshall is using our release actions with the hands spaced apart. Since the arms do not roll over the likelihood of a straight shot is greatly increased. With the hands separated on the club we can get a better understanding of the feel of the club swinging from the point of the arm shoulder triangle, with the right hand passing between the left hand and the ball. By allowing the left wrist to hinge, rather than roll over, through impact, the upper right arm (triceps) muscles and the forearm muscles of both arms can be used to their fullest without the fear of a hook. As will be learned within these pages; the forearms release the club with a twirling motion, the right arm throws and the wrists hinge sideways. The golf swing done this way allows a much more efficient application of power. This is a terrific drill, do it often.

Notice in the photo above that the clubface has not rotated around the shaft, instead the shaft has rotated beneath the wrists. Also that the butt end of the club has rotated in the opposite direction to the arc of the clubhead around the shaft at the X between the hands. For the clubhead to swing, the butt of the club must swing the opposite way. See the lower right photo on page 63. Notice also that the left hand is actually to the right of the right hand after impact (top right photo above), showing the complete release of the wrists. Tee up the ball when doing this drill and making sure that the clubface remains square swing it through. Using a tossing type motion of the right hand pass it between the left hand and the ball. Do not let the forearms roll over. As it swings, feel the blade work from closed to open.

THE FORMULA FOR POWER AND ACCURACY

The Helicopter

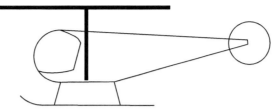

The sketch above depicts a helicopter, I chose this to illustrate more about the concept and actions of this golf swing. The reason I chose the helicopter is because it has 2 independent rotational centers as does the golf swing. The axle of the main rotor is one of these centers, the other is the axle of the tail rotor, together they produce pure flight.

So it is in the golf swing, the fuselage represents the left arm, it is turned by the main rotor shaft (the pivot), the tail rotor of the helicopter is a separate rotational action as is the twirl of the clubhead by the hands.

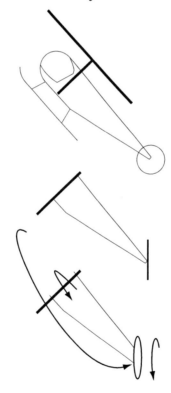

In the sketches above I have tilted the helicopter to represent the left arms angle. Next sketch down I have removed the unnecessary parts leaving only the fuselage (left arm), the main rotor shaft axle (the spine) and the tail rotor, the twirled club. The bottom sketch illustrates our concept, the fuselage is rotated by the main rotor as the tail rotor spins, together they produce the combined speed and power of both rotations.

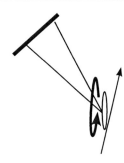

In the sketch above I show the fuselage in a stationary position, the tail rotor is spinning at a rapid rate. Notice that the tail rotor is rotating vertically and that anything the blades struck would be propelled rapidly in a straight line.

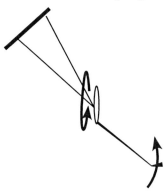

In the sketch above I have replaced the tail rotor with a golf club, its rotation is the same as the rotation depicted in the bottom sketch on the previous page. If balls were struck each time the club came around all would fly far and straight and would land very close together. If we were to speed up the tail rotor the balls would go farther and farther.

A point I wish to make clear here is that it is very difficult to speed up the left arm as we rotate through the shot. However it is relatively easy to increase the speed of the clubs rotation, this is the reason that we twirl the club rather than attempt to hit with it. This type rotation produces total accuracy by keeping the clubface square. Adding the pivot of the body adds power without hurting accuracy.

When we learn to speed up the pivot and also speed up the twirl of the club we begin to realize the true potential of this swing. Accuracy is assured so long as the pivot returns the left arm and clubhead down the correct path. Adding the vertically oriented twirl keeps the clubhead square so that the ball flies straight. The distance comes from the speed of the twirl combined with the power of the pivot. Simple to do once learned. The next 4 pages show more about this with sketches.

THE FORMULA FOR POWER AND ACCURACY

Front View Of The Fuselage And Club

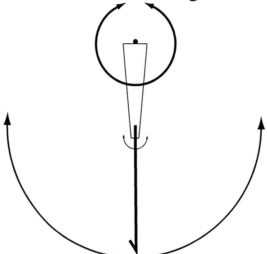

This series of sketches shows the relative actions of the left arm and the club. Above we have the address position, the club is in line with the left arm. Below we see the club already beginning to get behind the point of the triangle (one side missing). This also is the condition we will have at impact, the club will be about this much short of getting in line with the left arm. Point O shows the irons are impacted on the downward part of the arc. Point X shows that the driver is impacted on the upward part of the arc.

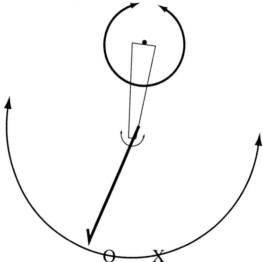

This sketch shows the down under and up actions of the fuselage, wrists and the golf club. The action is a scoop that catches the ball before the bottom of the arc with the irons, and slightly after the bottom of the arc with the driver, this allows us to hit the ball on the correct part of the arc of the clubs travel. With the irons the ball is struck before the ground eliminating fat shots. Off the tee the ball flies high with a low lofted driver. The ideal impact angle would have the shaft of the club just a tiny bit not quite caught up to the left arm, but coming fast and passing the left arm allowing the full release of energy.

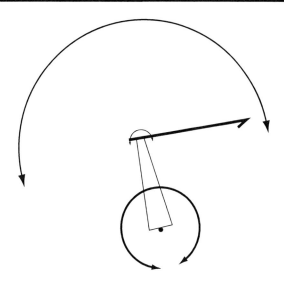

This is the mental picture of where we want to be at the top of the back swing. Due to the wind up of the forearms the blade will not be as shut as drawn, but slightly open (about 45 deg) to the shaft, but that opening motion occurred a long way from the ball and will be naturally returned as the forearms unwind coming back long before impact.

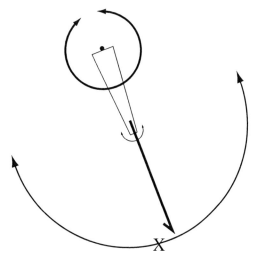

This is the mind picture we want as to where the club actually catches up and reaches the in line condition with the left arm. Notice, that with the driver it is soon after impact. With the wedge that has the impact earlier due to ball position and angle of attack, it would catch up later after the impact and divot. From here on till the top of the finish position the clubhead leads the way. It virtually pulls the arms around and up and helps the body regain the slight loss of balance that it loses as the clubhead pulls the body down and forward. Done properly the club feels like it is trying to pull your arms out of the shoulder sockets. Long drive champions report that they feel as if they were holding back a large angry dog on a chain momentarily as the club passes this point.

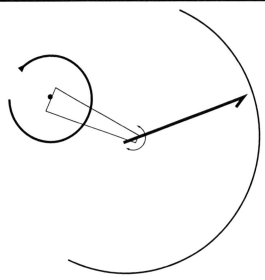

The right arm is straight from just after impact to the top of the finish as it takes over the role that the left arm had in the back swing only in reverse. The right arm controls the radius of the hand arc, the left arm simply folds and gets out of the way. The left arm actions are the exact reverse of the right arms back swing motions, the left elbow folds to allow the full release of the twirl as it swings out of the way as the left upper arm opens out.

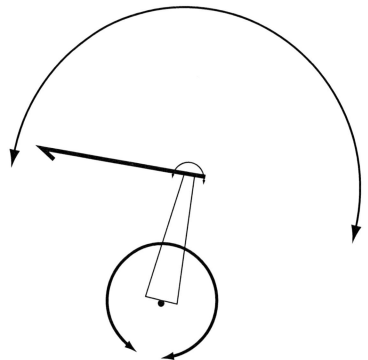

The finish is simply a reaction to all of the things that we did to swing the club, It is a gradual slowing down of all of the left over energy. Depending on the speed that you generate you may have the club hit your back or it may merely stop at the top.

The Tail Rotor

A way of understanding the movement of the club around the wrists as it is twirled on its way back to the ball can be found in the following sketch series of the tail rotor.

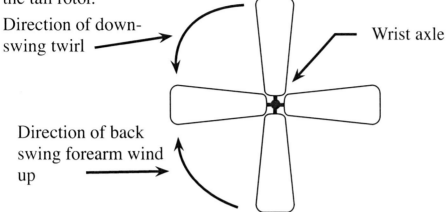

Direction of down-swing twirl

Wrist axle

Direction of back swing forearm wind up

The control of the direction and speed of the rotor uses a mental switch that reverses the direction and a rheostat that controls the speed. The wind-up and unwinding forearms you will learn in the arm movements create the same rotation.

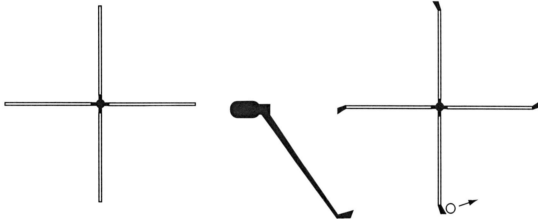

Here we have replaced the blades with shafts, angled out from the hub at the angle of an iron as can be seen in the center sketch. This is how our release operates, as can easily be seen the ball could only fly straight, since the club-faces never rotate around the shaft. The distance that the golf ball would fly would be controlled by the speed of the blades. If the center of the rotors rotation were still ball after ball could be sent the same distance and with the same direction and trajectory. To make the ball go farther would be a simple matter of increasing the speed of the whirling blade by turning up the rheostat. In our golf swing we increase the speed of the twirl and we also swing the whole assembly around with the pivot. For more power increase both speeds. It is important to note that it is extremely difficult to speed up the standard pivot that uses chest rotation, but it is relatively easy to speed up the twirl, and the late hip turn of our pivot. To see a human do it turn the page.

This photo series shows that it can be done by children as well as adults, G.J. Sanati is 11 years old, he plays extremely well after very little training. Notice the size of his swing arc in this series. His golfing future is bright.
He already is making an excellent swing that will last a lifetime.

The positions seen in this series of photos can be used as a template for your swing, if you compare your own swing to his through photographs. Just getting to these positions will help your swing. Above right G.J. has not quite gotten to the top of the back swing. Notice that at this point in his back swing the clubface appears shut, it is square to the ball. Beyond this point in the back swing the continued forearm wind-up actions slightly open the face, far from

Notice the position of the chest relative to the hips in these 2 photos, as can be seen the right hip, knee and the hands go through together. The hips are 45 degrees ahead of the chest. The actions of the legs have returned the arms. In the right photo the hinged spoke of the left arm and the club have returned to straight. As shown by the bowed right wrist, and cupped left wrist in the photo (below right); the right hand passes the left hand through impact and gets in front of, and then on top of, it.

Above left, G.J. has fully released the club and the speeding clubhead has pulled him to the top of the finish position, notice that the clubface has not rotated. Beyond this point the clubface again opens slightly, again far from the ball. The photos show that the body has moved only a small amount after impact, while the arms have swung quite a lot. Showing how much work was done by the legs prior to impact. The trunk muscles only release to allow the arms to swing through.

THE FORMULA FOR POWER AND ACCURACY

The Club, The Arms And The Body

The swing you will be learning in this book can be understood more simply when broken into components, three major units each with a separate job to do.

The first unit, I will call Unit # 1, is the golf club and the hands. The hands will be seen both as a part of the club, since they move with it, and a moving connection to the point of the triangle (Unit #2) at the wrist joints. The hands and club will both swing like a pendulum attached to the point of the triangle. The hands will not hit the ball, they will twirl the club in a cone, the clubhead will hit the ball, like a hammer hits a nail. Although travelling in a vertically oriented circle, the clubhead will hit the ball squarely and straight down the target line.

Unit # 2 is comprised of the shoulders, arms, elbows and again the hands. I refer to these parts as the triangle. This triangle is driven in a circular manner by the actions of Unit # 3, the pivoting body. The center of the triangles rotation is the upper end of the spine at the 7th cervical, a point centered between the shoulders. The triangle provides additional power to the circular twirl of the club as it turns, through the actions of its levers, as it shortens and lengthens the sides of the rotating triangle. The triangle also contains an additional action, the rotation of the forearm bones. The extension of the collapsed side of the triangle thus adds force to the returning speed of the triangle's point, as the twirling actions of the hands and forearms increase clubhead speed, around that point. By doing so it also controls the squareness of impact of Unit # 1 as well as providing the free swinging release of the twirled clubheads energy through the ball. The free swing of the release is vital.

Unit # 3 is the rest of entire body, minus the triangle and club. The use of the weight shift and pivot powers and rotates the other two units while maintaining the exact location of the upper end of the spine at the swing circle center. The swing circle center is the largest bump (7th cervical) at the top of the spine between the shoulder blades, the spine above that point is the neck. This point acts like a fulcrum to support the leverage of the top bar of the triangle, and also as a rotational center. The maintenance of a stationary swing circle center is vital, since it locates the center of the arcs of the other units, guaranteeing the correct return location of the clubhead to the ball. The better the stability of the center of the arcs, the simpler it is to meet the ball with the sweet spot of the club. Solid golf shots and consistent ball flight require the contact to be on the sweet spot, with the clubface square, anything else diminishes power, and usually direction as well.

The function of the neck is also independent, it supports the head as the body rotates. The head does not move relative to the ball and the flight line. Instead it actually rotates in the opposite direction of the chest rotation thus remaining still.

How We Do It
UNIT # 1
The Wrists and the Conical Release

THE FORMULA FOR POWER AND ACCURACY

Why The Club Swings Differently

This chapter begins the learning with a review of The Little Shot, to help those who have not studied the other book, for those who have a re-read of these improved pages will remind you of what the club must do through impact.

The goal of all golf swings is to make the club return perfectly through the ball. Yet mainstream instructors, at every level, teach a swing action that alters the relationship between the clubface and the ball. This causes the player to need to undo these alterations on the downswing. One of the largest visible differences between this swing and the other types of swings, is that through impact you will not use a motion that causes the clubface to rotate around the shaft. As stated previously, the commonly accepted wrist and arm movements cause the clubface to revolve around the shaft while the wrists cock up and down. At the same time, the arms also rise and lower from the wrists and shoulder sockets. These things change the clubs relationship, both to the body and the ball, by causing the clubhead to change planes. If that's not complex enough due to the roll of the forearms the clubface also opens and closes.

In this swing you will do none of the above.

Swinging with the commonly used swing is like playing Russian Roulette since the player is never really sure if his timing will be perfect enough to produce square contact. In this swing we will maintain the club-ball alignments set at address, simplifying solid contact and preserving shot predictability, yet hitting with increased power. It is the only true single plane swing.

This swing is also designed to keep the clubface from rolling open. Rolling open is what happens naturally as the right arm bends at the elbow, if we don't compensate for it with a slight forearm counter rotation. By today's standards "natural" is a synonym for good. Here, it can be done without.

Remember the plague is also "natural."

As the club swings through impact the wrists hinge sideways, a movement which has been considered taboo for years. This full swing release will be learned and practiced in the shot I call "The Little Shot", this release must be totally understood or our concept will be flawed. The photos on the opposite page (top) show what the clubface and clubhead must not do as the club passes through the hit. The photos (below) show what they do, although not quite as suddenly. The advantage direction wise is obvious, the difference in power delivery, once felt, will be equally dynamic.

What This Hand Action Allows

These photos show that any rolling action of the shaft does not advance the blade, instead it opens and closes it. When the club releases as shown in the photos below the wrists can function as axles and allow the shaft to pass under the forearms as it completely releases its energy into the ball. As can be seen in the 2 bottom photos the wrist can remain vertical and yet swing the club from behind the hand to in front of it. Part of this movement occurs in the full swing release as the club hits the ball.

Notice that by doing this the forearm bones do not roll in the hit area and can remain vertical as the club releases in a powerful slapping manner. This allows the right forearm to hit powerfully and accurately. Notice in the photos above that the butt end of the shaft passes under the forearms, as the hand slaps through. This action powerfully advances the clubhead and launches the ball.

THE FORMULA FOR POWER AND ACCURACY

The Actions Of The Hands

Due to the design of the wrist and forearm, the hand can move in many ways. We will make them work as if the wrist were a horizontal axle, to have better control of them. They can work as an axle no matter the angle of the hand relative to the forearm. In the sketches below you can see how the wrist can raise or lower the hand without changing the position of the forearm bones.

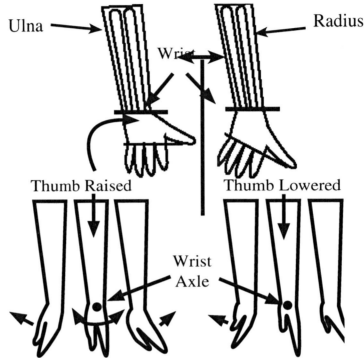

The hands on the left show the thumb in the lowered position, the hands on the right show the hands in the raised position. Due to the wrist's ability to rotate around the wrist axle the hands can release the club under the wrists regardless of the position of the hand relative to the forearm. This movement allows the hands to work in a car crank manner, shown on the following page, as we release the club. Also, due to this ability, all our clubs swing with the same arm action. The steep shaft angle of the wedges, or the flatter shaft angle of the driver and long irons, will not require any change in the swing action other than maintaining the wrist angle set at address. Using the wrists in this manner eliminates the difficulty of controlling the otherwise unruly wrists.

This releasing action begins just before the hands pass through impact. The hands only move about 45 degrees during this action. This action is a portion of, and is contained within, the forearm unwind soon to be studied. The release of the club in this manner keeps the clubface square to, and travelling straight down, the flight line. It creates shots without curvature and with great height.

The Car Crank Action Of The Wrists

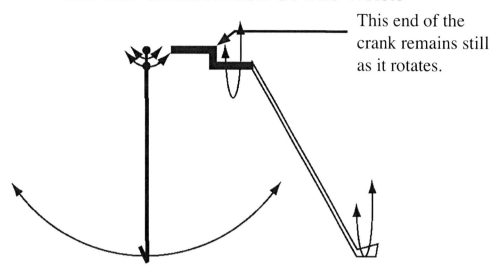

This end of the crank remains still as it rotates.

The sketch above shows a club with a crank handle, this illustrates part of the concept. The black circles at the top of the shaft represent the wrist axles. Since the right hand is below the left on the grip, when we use our wrist axles in the direction of the arrows the clubhead swings down under and up. Since the right hand wrist axle is below the left hand axle, the wrists work around the axles regardless of the hand angles, the hands then operate like a crank as they release. This action keeps the clubface square to the flight line, increasing accuracy and allowing extremely solid, square contact. Doing this the shaft swings in a cone.

The radius from the left wrist axle to the clubhead determines the clubheads arc and distance of travel. The radius of the right wrist, from the wrist axle to the base of the fingers, rotates under the left wrist axle just as a crank would. This type of release both increases the space where the clubface is square to the target and at the same time frees-up the swinging clubhead. The hands and the club must freely swing beneath the wrist axles just as a pendulum does beneath a clock. For this to occur; the arms must relax and allow the unwind of the forearms, together with centrifugal force and gravity, to swing the pendulum as the right arm hits through and the wrists release. Power is added by a tossing type right forearm movement, thus allowing the use of the powerful inner right forearm muscle. The clubhead is then directed and controlled for squareness by the vertical left forearm as the right hand and forearm throw it through.

Correctly done the wrist angles and the wind-up of the forearms as we make our back swing will control the correct position of the clubface as the club reacts to centrifugal force, gravity and the unwinding of the forearms through impact.

THE FORMULA FOR POWER AND ACCURACY

The Conical Release

In this method, you are learning a release that keeps the face of the club both traveling along the line and square to it much longer.

To accomplish this here is a unique way to swing the clubhead through the ball. In this method the club shaft, due to the wrist crank motions, rotates a small amount in the exact opposite direction of the forearm roll in the common swing release, this action keeps the clubface square through the hit area of the swing.

We will begin to learn this release with a chip shot that I call "The Little Shot". In this shot you will swing the clubhead through the ball while controlling the clubface with the forearms. The club will swing in a cone.
  But before we do, let's see why this is important to learn.

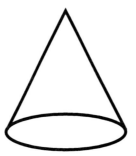

A WEIGHT SWINGING IN A CIRCLE FROM A TACK
IN THE CEILING PRODUCES A CONE

The above sketch shows how a weight could swing from a tack in the ceiling, in a circle that is parallel to the floor, Due to this the combination of the circle, and the arc described by the string, is a cone. So it is with the club, our clubhead travels in a circle, but the shaft, as it swings from the wrists, follows a cone.

The motions soon learned in the little shot will train the hands and forearms to swing the club in this conical action. Working in this fashion the release of the wrists will cause a perfectly controlled vertical circular arc of the clubhead, around the tip of the arm shoulder triangle, within the full swing. Releasing this way will allow the use of all of our forearm and hands strength and also their speed, to increase the speed of the clubhead. It is their correct use that gives much clubhead speed with true clubface control.

This release action, when used in the full swing, is very free, powerful and extremely accurate.

When the hands move the club in a cranking fashion the clubhead swings in a conical action. By swinging this way, the clubface passes through the ball in a more precise and powerful manner.

This conical movement, when combined with the forearm wind up and the pivot, keeps the clubface on plane and square to the ball throughout 90% of the entire swing. The 5 percent of the swing where the clubface is not square to the ball is at the ends of each half of the swing (the top of the back swing and the end of the follow through). These places are far from the ball, and so have no effect.

How We Do It
UNIT # 1
The Little Shot

Training The Hands

An extremely important part of the body motion in this golf swing is the, through impact, release actions of the hands. They should be trained, early and often, as you are learning this method. The actions of the hands and club in the photo series on the following pages, both create and train a conical action of the club so vital to this swing. These hand actions train the down under and up action of the releasing clubhead in the full swing. Once learned with a practice shot I call, "The Little Shot" or the 1/8 shot. This movement of the hands and club is an integral part of what happens in a full drive. The way that the club swings through the hit of "The Little Shot" occurs within every full swing with every club.

One of the earliest hand actions can best be described as a slight counter-clockwise twist of the shaft. This is done by tucking the left pinky knuckle as the right wrist sets straight back. This twisting action will cause the clubface to only de-loft, not roll open, it can be seen in the photo on the facing page. The triangle of the arms, elbows and shoulders (Unit #2) does not move. Nor does the body (Unit #3) The motion is done only by the hands from the wrist axles. The point of the triangle must remain fixed in space relative to the ball. If the hands move away from the starting point you are doing this drill wrong. Done correctly the blade or face of the club will remain square to the flight line. **The clubhead will not swing in, instead it will go straight back and up with the sweet spot of the clubface staying directly centered on, and square to, the flight line.** See the photo series on the following pages. The importance of grooving the slight shaft twist and right wrist set cannot be over stated. Take your time and get it right, it is the key that unlocks solid contact.

This drill trains the beginning of the conical action of the back swing, notice that the shaft only moves 45 degrees, if it moves further you are doing it wrong. Swinging through it also goes past center only 45 degrees. This action creates an accurate chip shot, since the ball can only go straight, however it should only be attempted in play when the lie is very good and the shot is very short. When doing this type chip in play the clubhead is only powered and moved by the relatively weak forearm muscles. The clubhead is also moving quite slowly, due to this any resistance encountered in the hit, such as catching stiff grass, or hitting a tiny bit fat will weaken the hit enough to spoil the shot. We will modify this chip action in play by hitting to the ball with the hands and firming the grip just before contact. The hands will then be locked and forward of the contact point at impact. The hands will not release fully, the shaft and clubhead will lock and move forward with the left arm. This will make the hit less likely to be weakened by unwanted ground or grass contact since the club and left arm will then be a long solid lever.

Twisting The Shaft And Setting The Right Wrist

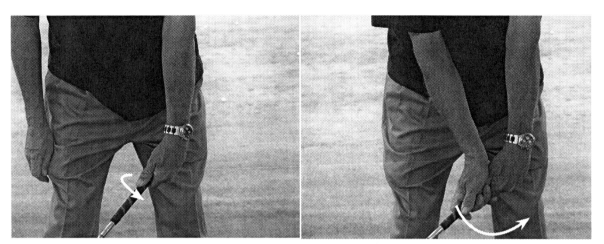

Here are the earliest hand actions described on the facing page. In the photo on the left is the pinky tuck and twist that moves the shaft 45 degrees. Done correctly it does not rotate the forearm bones. This movement is caused by a tuck of the left pinky knuckle, it should feel as if you are twisting the grip a small amount in a counter-clockwise direction. The photo above right shows the cocking back action of the right wrist that goes with it. From here it is simple to see how the right hand could hit the ball, simply by moving as the arrow indicates.

These very important movements, they set the hands and with them the clubface into a position that when used with the rest of the arm actions creates the conical action which in turn creates solid club ball contact and perfect shots.

I repeat, "this hand action will cause the clubface to remain square to the flight line and keep the sweet spot of the club centered over it".

The hands thus control and power a conical, rotation of the clubhead as it makes an orbit around the hands. In the full swing this release, when combined with the other two Units, and the winding and unwinding forearms; are part of a double combination of arcs that blend together to create the tremendous speed of the clubhead with perfect clubface control through impact.

The first arc is vertical one created by the conical rotation of the club around the hands. The hands (Unit # 2) are rotated in a totally different arc by the pivot of the body (Unit # 3), around the swing circle center. It is the combination of these two separate yet perfectly controlled coinciding circular arcs that create the clubhead arc, on the oblique plane that create the power and the accuracy so necessary for perfect golf shots.

We start the, "Little Shot," chip drill in the normal address position. The weight is 90 percent on the left heel. The only weight on the right foot, is the weight of the lower right leg and the right foot.

Moving only the hands, not the chest, legs or arms, set the clubhead back by tucking the left pinky knuckle under. As seen in the photo above Point X must not move. The body weight must remain on the left foot.

Correctly done the clubhead will follow a conical arc; it will remain square to, above and centered on, the flight line. As shown here by the club on the ground. The toe of the club would slide in a cone against a wall, were it touching one.

At address the club has normal loft, or what ever loft you may choose to set it to by leaning the shaft forward. You can choose to hit a lower than normal shot this way, or open the face for more loft, with also more pinch.

Here Jim has moved the center of the triangle to the right by bending the right elbow. Notice the hands have left point X, this is a movement we must not do as we learn this shot. The club may not return to the same spot, and the ball will go too far.

If point X does not move at impact the release actions of the wrists automatically return the club to what ever angles you set at address. Beyond impact the clubface lays back in the conical release. Going through the **right** pinky knuckle tucks increasing the loft. This appears to be a scooping action, but since the ball is hit on the way down with the hands forward of the ball, this is not a scoop.

This left hand action, demonstrated by Mike Foster, as the forearms wind going back and unwind going through, keep the shaft from rolling as the club passes through impact. The left wrist release action (arrow, photo above), is needed to allow the toss of the clubhead underhand with the right hand. This action guides the clubheads path and arc and stabilizes it with the left hand. This simple wrist release action considered taboo for years by mainstream golf instruction is part of what makes this swing work so well.

The right hand cannot throw through if this left hand release does not happen. Notice that the left hand fist knuckles rotate down under and up. Notice in the photo below how the left palm faces down after impact, as the full swing continues from this point the left thumb would get behind and under the shaft. When this action is done in the full swing, the knuckles of the left hand will lead the follow through simply by following the arc that they are moving in (arrow, photo below).

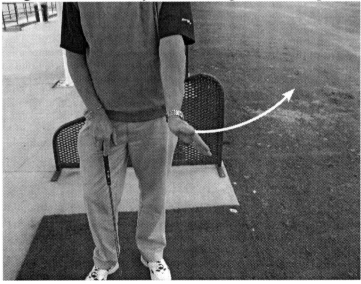

Right and Wrong

The top photo on the facing page shows the correct left hand motion for setting the wrist cock and releasing the club under. Notice that the forearm bones do not rotate open or closed as in the photos below. As seen in the photos (opposite page) the left wrist gets a slight bow, in the larger swings as the right elbow gets involved this slight bow will almost disappear due to the point of the triangle moving right of the center of the chest. At the top of the back swing the left wrist must still have a very slight bow, for it to release. It cannot release properly if the wrist is cupped.

The photo, top left facing page, also shows the classic raised wrist bone at impact taught by Ben Hogan. Since his teachings were taken at face value the roll over of the forearms has been adapted. In this swing the wrist is not frozen, it is releasing like a hinge and continues un-hinging through to the finish. Using this movement allows the right wrist to throw the clubhead through the ball as it releases the pendulum for greater impact and height. This keeps the forearms from rolling over and eliminates a possible hook. This action launches the ball up and causes it to fly dead straight. It allows complete use of all of the right arms power with control. I believe this motion was a secret he never revealed, but used in his own swing, hence his accuracy.

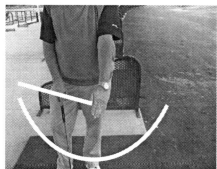 

The photos above show what we **don't want the hands to do**.
Notice that although the thumbs have moved the same 45 degrees, the motion was done by turning the forearm bones rather than allowing the club to swing under. Since the palm of either hand is the same as the clubface this action opens and closes the clubface. Once opened it must be returned to square to produce a straight shot. This is the way the club is swung in the common swing, the wrists have to cock up, not under, by raising the thumbs. This also raises the clubhead and alters the plane of the clubheads arc, creating more complication. This type action requires a reverse of the forearm opening roll to hit the ball straight, and the hands must un-cock the clubhead back down to the on plane position for impact. Any return not perfectly timed causes a less than perfect shot.

When the hands are set and released as shown on the previous page the club will swing straight down the line with a square clubface, in the perfect release arc.

THE FORMULA FOR POWER AND ACCURACY

Once the wrists have set the club you should find that the shaft has moved almost exactly 45 degrees to the right as in the top right photo on page 48, not farther away as in the top right photo on page 49. If the club swings this far back either the left wrist over-cocked or the point of the triangle has moved or both. If it goes beyond 45 degrees relative to the hands the right elbow will have flexed. It will flex in larger shots, but must not in this one. To train the hands we must not do either of those things. The chest and feet also do not move, the weight remains on the left leg at all times. Remember this drill is to train the hands to rotate under the wrist axles, the right hand must pass between the left hand and the ball as the right hand hits through as in the lower right photo on page 49. Notice that the clubface has increased the loft (laid back) not rolled closed. The feel is of the right pinky knuckle tucking under, this movement is the reverse of the left pinky tuck that started the shot. It creates the crank action conical release.

Begin learning this shot with your sand wedge, the shot should only travel about 10 yards or 1/8 as far as you hit the club. Later on learn the little shot on all your irons, as you practice on the longer clubs pay close attention to the trajectory, carry and roll distance that you get with each club. This knowledge will be very helpful when you need to hit a lower flying chip with more run out.

This drill should be done for at least 20 shots every time that you begin your practice session, the drill will soon be perfected. In 30 days or less the balls will fly straight and stop very close to each other. After that the drill should still be done for a few balls at the start of every warm up. The importance of learning this drill cannot be overstated, it is how well you learn this release action in the little shot that determines how well you will do it in full shots when the club is travelling at a very high rate of speed. It is much easier to train the motions of the hands while they are moving relatively slowly, and are under conscious control, than when they are reacting to gravity and are following a grooved pattern. This drill trains the wrists to move, not freeze.

Practicing this shot, is the training of the pattern of the release the hands will follow without conscious control during play. This action must be ingrained in muscle memory, so that it requires no conscious control during play. The final release of the hands in the full shots, must be turned over to the forces of nature (Centrifugal Force and Gravity) plus the natural contraction of the muscles we stretched as we made our back swing. When we let the clubhead fully release with relaxed hands and wrists the naturally returning muscles guide the hit. Until this underneath release happens naturally we will make it happen to groove the action.

THE 21st CENTURY GOLF SWING

Assisting The Release

Early on in our training of the hands we may need to help the clubhead release beyond the point of the triangle. It should be fairly easy to make the release happen with the little shot and the slightly larger shots soon to come. However it may be more difficult for you to do on full hard shots, due to the natural tightening of the hands as we hit the ball. Here is a little trick that you should start using in the little shot practice sessions that will help groove it for the larger shots. Later on if you find the clubhead not penetrating the ball well, on fuller shots, use this trick to make it happen there too.

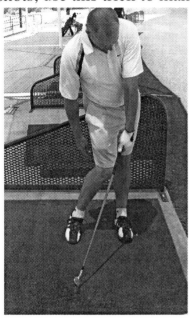 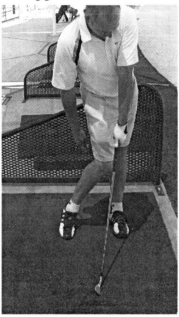 

In the photos above we see the club arriving with the left wrist slightly bowed, ala Ben Hogan. As the hands move the clubhead through impact we use both the inner forearm muscle of the right arm in a tossing manner, and the outside muscles of the left forearm (arrow in right photo) to assist the swinging action.

The tossing action will feel quite natural and easy to do right away, since we have all used it many times in our lives. The left hand action is not commonly done, it should feel like a combination of turning the knuckles up toward the target and the way you would turn your arm to look at the back of your glove.

Practice this releasing action with both hands, and with each hand separately. In a short amount of time you should be able to hit the little shot equally well with either hand or both together. This hand release must cause the clubhead to follow the conical arc, the clubhead should go straight down the flight line and remain above it throughout its travel as if the toe of the clubhead touches an imaginary wall, the lines on the blade must remain perpendicular to that wall.

UNIT #1
Twirling The Club

THE FORMULA FOR POWER AND ACCURACY

Rotary Versus Lineal

The golf club must move either lineally or in a rotary fashion, it cannot do both.

The common swing conception is of rotating the arm and shoulder lever assembly around the swing circle center while maintaining the wrist cock, thus bringing the club endwise (lineally). This concept teaches a delay in releasing by holding the wrist angles in the uncocked position until late in the downswing to change a lineal movement into rotary motion as the angle snaps open. This action does add some clubhead speed by creating the late release we have all heard so much about, but requires hand eye coordination and timing to square the blade. Thus only those blessed with these gifts can do it consistently.

We, instead, will be making the club move in a purely rotary fashion throughout the golf swing. Our golf swing also has a late release, but it is not due to attempting to hold on to anything. The release in this swing will start at the top of the downswing and continue uninterrupted to the top of the finish. The hands arms and forearms will be applying power to the rotary moving club from the beginning of the downswing all of the way through the hit to the end of the finish. The late release will be executed through the hit as our right arm extends and the right hand tosses through as it passes between the left hand and the ball. There will be no need to consciously control this late hit action, it is simply a part of the entire sequence of the rotary forearm unwind action. The release action will feel slow, but the clubhead speed will be very fast.

The difference in the amount of power that can be supplied is akin to the difference in distance one can obtain from throwing a ball versus throwing a ball out the window of a rapidly moving train.

We will be swinging the clubhead in a true circle relative to the wrists as the pivot returns the rotating forearms around their orbit, these 2 divergent circles by blending together will both create the speed of the clubhead and the correct path of the club. These actions combined with the correct forearm unwind cause the clubhead to release through impact with no shaft rotation. The path and the plane as well as the squareness of the clubface will be controlled perfectly. The shots will fly true with pure backspin if you so desire, or with some side spin as well if that is what you intend. This will allow you to influence either the balls curvature in flight and / or its bounce after landing.

The Visual Difference

In this sketch we have a club launched by an angry golfer in a lineal fashion, it is traveling endwise from point A to point B. Even though the arc is a curving one the club does not exhibit rotary motion. If the club were to hit the ground somewhere after point B, where the shaft had rotated more vertically due to the downward arc caused by gravity the motion could change to a rotary one as the club ended up twirling around a fixed point (as in point X in the sketches below).

Here we have another club, this one launched in a rotary motion by our angry golfer, as can be seen in the sketches even though the club is travelling from right to left across the page it is rotating around a fixed point, X).

THE FORMULA FOR POWER AND ACCURACY

Twirling The Club

The way that the club swings in this method is entirely different and in order to do it you need a different concept of what you are doing and why you are doing it. The club spins around the point of the triangle in a circle as the shaft describes a cone. Twirling the head of the club in this vertical circle will be done with a hand action that approximates the twirling of a baton. Rather than simply using a right arm extension (thrust) type effort to swing the club, instead we add speed to the clubhead similar to the way a key ring is swung. Adding this action to the straightening and throwing actions of the right arm adds much power.

A baton twirling type action will give us an action of the club that is entirely rotary around the wrists. As you will see in the following sketches and descriptions, its motion will be an entirely independent action from the pivot which comprises the rest of the body actions, less the arms and shoulders. It is however an integral part of the actions of the triangle as the sides shorten and lengthen.

In the common golf swing concept the club is kept from releasing early in the downswing and the opening of the angle is delayed in order to increase the whip of the release. Totally unlike that concept, in this golf swing there is never any attempt to bring the club endwise toward the ball (lineal motion, see sketches page 57). In this swing we consciously delay nothing, as a matter of fact we begin adding speed to the clubhead immediately by twirling it (rotary motion) and actually hit the ball starting right from the top. Doing this gives a large head start in creating clubhead speed, this equals power.

The final release of the wrist still occurs very late in the action in a tossing type wrist action, but it is done automatically as the wrist axles release.

The club is thus given additional power by the down under and up clubhead arc. Due to the twirling / throwing motion, we create much centrifugal force, which is further assisted by gravity and the power of the pivot.

The combination of the twirling action of the forearms and the natural straightening actions of the right arm create speed. The controlled path of the clubhead caused by the pivot, sends the clubhead through the ball absolutely square, and facing down the flight line through a large release arc. It will also possess much speed, yet will not feel as if the action took a lot of effort. This collection of motions, properly executed, unlock the power and the accuracy of this golf swing.

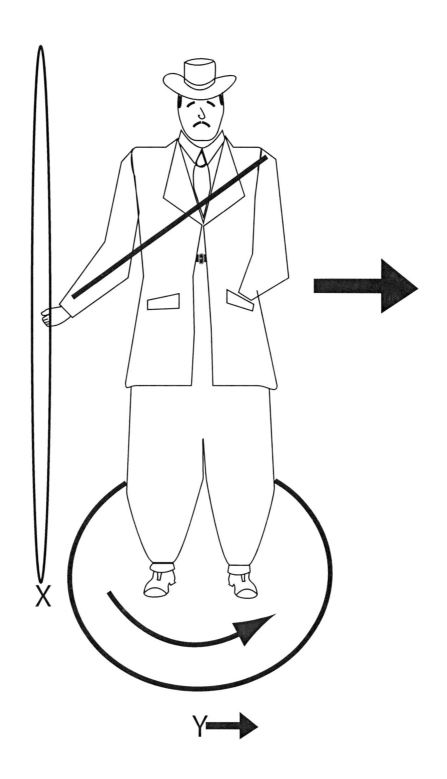

X

Y→

Spinning The Key Ring

On the preceding and facing pages we have a Zoot Suiter spinning a key ring, the keys are coming from behind him under and up, just like the lasso. He is spinning the keys on the right side of his body out in front of his body. If the keys kit the ground at point X (pg. 59) the sparks would fly toward you. With a very small amount of physical effort he can spin the keys at a very high rate of speed. If the keys were of sufficient weight the impact of it hitting a passerby would be painful. This underhand spinning rotation is the key to understanding the use of the forearms and the way we add speed and power to the clubhead and from there into the ball.

As can be seen in the sketches, he is standing on a manhole cover. If the manhole cover were to suddenly rotate in the direction of the arrow it is easy to see that the keys would strike the ground at point Y, assuming that they reached the bottom of the arc when the turn reached 90 degrees. At that point he would be facing in the direction of the large black arrow and his keys would be swinging in the direction of the small black arrow at the wrist. The letter Y would then be propelled in the same direction. If it were a golf ball and the keys were the clubhead it would produce a shot straight toward the target. The black line (pg 59) and grey sleeve (pg 61) across the chest represents the position of a golfers left arm at impact. Both forearms rotate in the same direction as the keys. Read this line again it is not a misprint.

If the speed of the rotation of the keys and the manhole cover were synchronized each time he reached point Y the keys would also reach that point.

The impact would be the combined force of the speed of the twirl plus the speed of the manhole covers rotation, for more power we could increase the speed of the twirl only but it would then be necessary to double it to insure that it hit the Y on the second rotation to time it perfectly. It is far easier to increase both speeds so that each is turning at a similar rpm. The golfer has an easier time of this due to the fact that the club has a shaft rather than a key chain and the clubhead can be influenced at the start of the downswing by an applied force. Later in the swing the speed of the clubhead is greatly increased by the whip like force created by the combined forces of centrifugal force and gravity as the clubhead accelerates to reach its full extension. Its speed is so great that it passes the full extended position through impact. It is interesting to note that it is nearly impossible to hit too early.

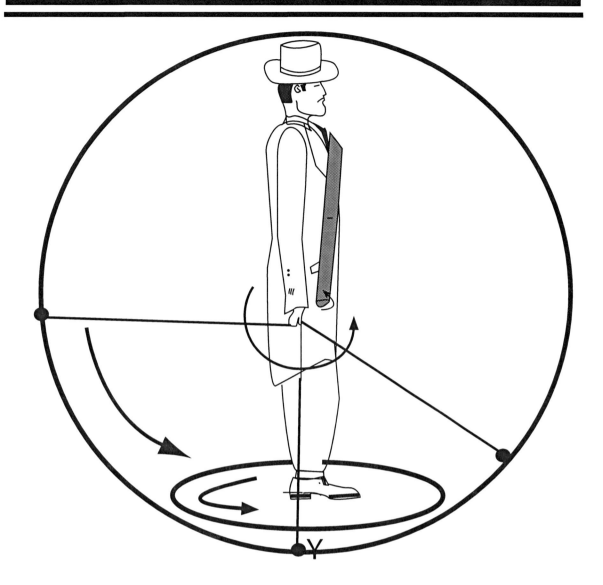

In the above sketch we see the key chain go down under and up as it illustrates the way we release the golf club through the conical arc.

If the golfers left arm were on the club, his left forearm must also revolve in the same direction as the wrist releases the club around the left wrist axle.

The tiny arrow around the gray left arm shows the counter-clockwise direction the left forearm revolves in to allow this to happen. The left palm will face downward after impact. The right forearm also rotates the same way, when both wrists do this it allows the club to swing under. If the left wrist does not flex (release) the right hand cannot hit through and it will then roll over and impart a hooking flight to the ball. Since both hands are on the club, whatever one hand does the other must mirror.

Down Under And Up

The sketch on the previous page shows the arc of the keys as they release, notice that the motion is down under and up rather than the out over and around direction of the clubhead in the common swing. Our club will release this way.

By swinging and releasing the club in this fashion much accuracy is gained since the clubhead is travelling straight down the line for a longer time and the blade or face of the club is not revolving around the shaft. For this type release to happen the hands must move in the motions seen in the photos on pages 67, 68 and 69.

The little club seen there is a tremendous training aid since it gives instant visual feed back as to what any hand movements do to the clubhead and clubface.

The learning of the hand actions can happen quickly with consistent practice of these motions over a period of several (4) weeks. It takes roughly 28 days to cement in a new habit pattern, do not overlook the importance of this, especially if you have a long history of doing it differently. Remember, it took you (depending on how long you are playing) months, years or perhaps decades to groove what you now do. Do not expect it to go away just because you now know what to do differently. It must be repeated until it replaces your old move.

Just as an obese person did not gain the excess weight in a short time, and must take a period of hard work to remove it, your release move will take 4 weeks of doing it perfectly to change. This is much like quitting smoking, forgetting to practice correctly or practicing incorrectly we become the person who sneaks one little cigarette after a day or two. Just as he has little chance of succeeding in his half-hearted quest to change his habits we will prolong how long it takes to groove our action.

As some wizened soul once said. "Practice does not make perfect, practice makes permanent. Perfect practice makes perfect."

To make a change requires discipline and attention to correctness, make it a good habit to get into this mental frame of mind each time you practice and you can change your action much more quickly than any other way. A player can not wish the way to success, but we can set a realistic goal and follow the path.

What Is Twirling?

We can generate a lot of speed by twirling a key ring, but how does this relate to swinging a club? This series of sketches describe what is happening as the club is twirled rather than used as a bludgeon to strike the ball. These sketches also tie together the concept of the conical action, later we will learn of the swing away and return of this center of the club twirl, (the rotating point of the triangle brought by the pivot) and the twirling action of the club.

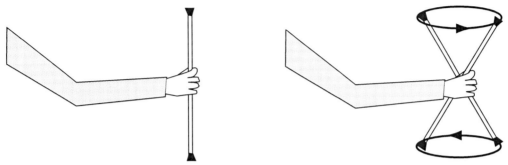

Above we have a hand holding a baton, we have all seen how they can be twirled. The top right sketch shows a bit of how a twirl can be made. Notice that the ends of the baton make equal sized circles, one above the hand and one below the hand. These motions create 2 cones, one above and one below the hand. The circles are the same size, rotating in opposite directions, since the hand is holding the baton in the center.

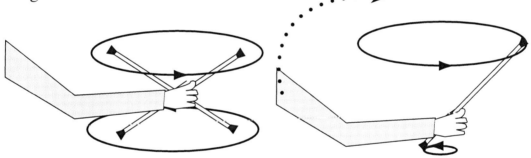

Above we can see how these circles (baton still held in the center) can be made larger as the wrist moves farther. The sketch on the right shows that if the baton is held off center one circle gets larger, the other smaller. Since we are twirling the club from near its upper end, the circle of the clubheads travel will be quite large. It is also important to notice that the twirled club is following the path described by the arrow. In other words by twirling the club we can cause it to travel in a flat circle, relative to the location of the center of the cone. If the sketch on the right were rotated 90 deg. clockwise (dotted arrow lower right photo) the arc would be vertical. **Notice that the top end of the club rotates in the opposite direction.** This action is very important to understand when we start swinging the club since by using it we can make very rapid clubhead speed, without much effort, and the clubhead will pass the hands automatically.

SPINNING A LASSO

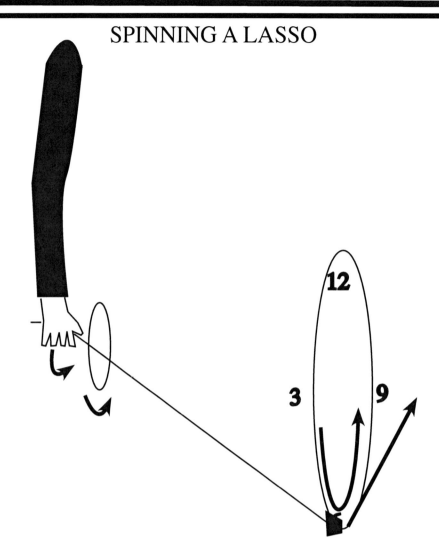

When a cowboy spins a lasso the knot can be seen travelling around the loop in a circle, the hand must rotate the rope in the same direction that the loop travels.

This is a good visual to the secret of the way our hand release works. The arc described by the knot is a circle, the sides of the arc of the rope to the hand describes a cone. Due to gravity this is impossible; when spinning a rope to get a cone the ground must be to the right of the photo, so that the weight of the spinning rope would cause it to be below the hand. If it were spun vertically as drawn, gravity would cause the hand to be at the circles center. However since the club has a shaft and not a rope it can swing in this conical manner, and it will have perfect directional control and with it the power of a crank.

Here the rotation is in a clockwise direction. Notice that the knot representing the clubhead travels down under and up and that it travels straight down the flight line. All of the arrows rotate in the same down under and up direction.

CLUB RELEASING IN LASSO MOTION

The release of the right wrist will be similar to the wrist motions necessary to spin a rope, it is a relaxed easy movement of the hand with the forearm muscles. When we swing a club (full swing) in this fashion, the right wrist will rotate the club through the entire cone. Here the bottom portion of the conical lasso's loop is where the wrist axles release our club through the impact area. The clubhead then revolves in the down under and up direction of the arrow using the conical, cranking type tossing hand release action. To do this it must wind up in a counter rotation going back, by turning the clubface under, and keep the face looking at the ball. It will continue under as the forearms wind. The forearms will continue the counter rotation wind-up all of the way to the top of the back swing. More on the wind up of the forearms on the coming pages.

THE FORMULA FOR POWER AND ACCURACY

The Full Windup Of The Forearms

In order to create a twirling action of the club around the point of the arm shoulder triangle we must first wind up the forearms in the reverse of the direction of the down swing twirl. The wrist actions, started in the little club right hand set, will now get additional help in powering the club, from a wind-up and unwind of the forearms.

The combination of the counter-rotation forearm windup with the tromboning action of the right arm put the right arm into the perfect throwing position and as we swing down that is exactly what we do. See the forearm wind up photo series on the facing page to get the complete understanding that only photos can give. Once the right wrist sets back the forearms both wind counter-clockwise, the club rotates around the right forearm as shown in the lower left photo (facing page). This counter rotation causes the right elbow to swing out to the perfect position.

When we wind the forearms in the described manner we bring into play many more forearm muscles. This use of more muscles, and very quick ones at that, lets us add more early clubhead speed. The early speed, combined with the pivot (Unit #3) and late right hand bowling ball release (page) creates maximum speed for a players available strength. Starting the downswing with an easy feeling twirl from the top of the back swing gives a head start on making clubhead speed.

This early start could be considered a cast by the uninformed, but since the left arm, as we use Unit #3, is also being quickly driven around by the actions of the feet, legs and hips, it is anything but. As a matter of fact it is what is necessary to make the club catch up to the left arm. If you do not twirl the club, as you extend the right arm and throw the clubhead through with the right hand it will likely not catch up.

Ideally the club has almost reached the straight in line with the left arm condition as the ball is impacted. The powerful twirl, the right arm straightening and the release with the left knuckles turning up, allows the club to swing unimpeded through the ball. The clubhead quickly passes the left arm and pulls the extended right arm through as it swings to a total release.

This total and complete release of the swinging pendulum of the club allows the club to also complete the release arc sooner. We are trying to make the clubhead reach the end of its extension just after impact and be starting to come back toward us while the hands are still going toward the target.
The laws of physics keep this from happening, but it must be our goal.

How It Looks When Done With The Little Club

The little club is an invaluable tool to learn the forearm windup, it gives instant feed back as to what happens to the clubhead as the hands make their motions. Remember the club swings in a cone even on this short club.

This photo series shows the complete movement of the club around the right forearm. The conical action of the club allows the forearm to duplicate what the club does in the full swing. The cocking of the wrist and counter rotation of the forearm are visibly apparent. This series of actions is exactly what the right hand does in the full swing. The motion of the releasing club is circular around the right forearm. The right forearm itself is brought around by the actions of the pivot. Make or purchase a little club so that you can practice this drill a lot, the twirl must be practiced until it is automatic, done properly this creates tremendous clubhead speed. Below, note the hand positions at the top and at finish.

Note; The right wrist is cocked fully back, and wound up, in position to twirl and throw.

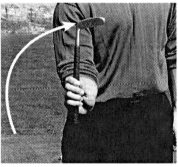 

Note; The right wrist is fully bowed, showing that the right hand has fully thrown through in a slapping manner.

The un-winding rotation of the right wrist sends the clubhead rapidly around the outside of the circle as the left arm is returned by the pivot. In this photo series notice that the clubhead makes the full circle. Practice until the arm rotation is so quick that the eye can't see it, when done EMPTY HANDED. Little clubs can be purchased through the web site aperfectswing.com or made by cutting down an old club. Where you get one does not matter, but get one. It will make the entire actions of the hands and the clubface both understandable as well as feel able. As in all physical actions feel is the true control. The wrist cocked and bowed positions are vital. The right hand must make this exact move as we swing.

Giving The Ball Extra Zip

The unwinding action of the forearms uses more muscles and is much quicker than a slapping motion alone. The photos below show how this happens.

The above photos show how the unwinding of the forearms blends into the flapping car crank wrist release. This movement is natural and feels easy.

The arrows in <u>all</u> of these photos go in the same direction.

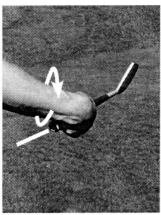 

Notice that the lower forearm bone has rotated under and forward of the upper forearm bone.

These photos show the continued release and the straight white line in the lower left photo shows how the shaft has passed under the forearms; it has allowed a full hit with the right hand without rolling the blade closed. The bottom right photo, shows the rest of the forearm unwind, completing the full circle of the swing. The motion is as if you open a door knob as you throw. It is clockwise!

This hand action is the key to making clubhead speed and controlling it. Do not take this twirling type hand and wrist action lightly, it must be understood, and practiced into a natural free wheeling action. It adds much speed and zip.

If you had a ping pong paddle in your hand you could hit the ball surprisingly hard and it would go away very quickly. This wrist action is commonly used by some world class ping pong players to create amazing ball speed. It works equally well when applied to the golf swing.

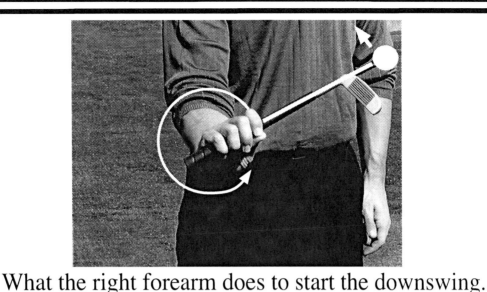

What the right forearm does to start the downswing.

Even though you are looking at the club from the front, the idea I am trying to convey is as if you were looking straight down at the right hand from directly above, since the right forearm is vertical and parallel to the spine, at the top of the back swing. If the fingers were open he could be holding a plate of spaghetti in the same plane that the rotating arrow shows. Notice that the player would be looking at quartering view of the back of the right forearm, the right palm would then be facing somewhat away from the player. The counter rotation and re-rotation of the right forearm duplicates the actions the club makes in the full swing.

Here I show the motion as we would twirl a ball on a string. A simple unwinding of the forearm would fling the meatballs off the plate or send the tethered ball rapidly around in a circular motion. This is exactly what the right arm does to start the clubhead on its journey around the outside of the downswing arc. This action starts the clubhead away from the direction the left arm is traveling and builds much clubhead speed. It should feel light and does not require much effort to perform. The effort is only for the first 1/4 of the forearm's rotation and then should be felt to free wheel as the right triceps straightens. The straightening right arm and the right forearm toss, then pass the shaft under the left hand in the car crank motion. If the shaft were choked up on a long club, the shaft would pass under the forearms as this happens, as in the lower left photo on the facing page.

After impact the left forearm continues the counter-clockwise rotation started by the right forearm. The left hand then attains the "Cop Saying Stop" position, (page 135). After impact, the left thumb will first get behind the shaft as the wrist axles rotate and then get under the shaft as the forearms continue to rotate, finishing in a position similar to the lower right photo facing page, but with a little less bow.

After The Hands Are Trained

The training of the hands and the actual use of the hands are slightly different from each other during actual golf shots. The drills train the wrists to release the club in a down under and up arc rather than a rolling closed clubface action.

Once this type release arc of the clubhead has been learned and the slight twist of the shaft that keeps the face square, yet has the leading edge of the club rotating under the face, in the back swing is grooved the hand and arm release you used to learn it will be slightly modified. This action uses the hands, elbows and shoulders, it lets you feel how they move but not where they move in the full swing. The left arm will remain back in the #7 position there (text page 74, pic page 93).

Start by slightly twisting the shaft in a counter-clockwise manner using only the left hand from below the wrist axle to the fist knuckles. As you do this focus on keeping the thumbs from lifting the clubhead, while swinging the arms from the shoulder sockets as the elbows hinge. We do this as the left arm moves to the right in an arc from the shoulder, and the right wrist sets fully back. The left palm feels to seek the right shoulder. As this happens the right elbow folds, this makes the large bow in the back of the left wrist become smaller visually.

The left wrist must have a slight bow, this bow is necessary to put the left hand into a position from which the wrist will not cock vertically very much. It will cock vertically a small amount, but only several degrees, rather than the full 90 degrees of wrist cock as done in the standard swing concept. This keeps the clubhead far away from the swing circle center, thus producing a larger arc. This action also does two other things, first it eliminates having to get the clubhead back down to the perimeter of the arc, since it never leaves it, second it forces the continued windup of the forearms to get the club into the correct top of the back swing position. Once wound, they are then in a position to unwind. Going through the opposite actions occur.

Even though this is a modification to our initial movements, the wrist axles will still function in the manner already trained but will feel to be much slower in their actions. The clubhead movement however will be anything but slow.

Once felt the hand actions and elbow movements will feel to be much more controlled and the entire action of the upper triangle and club assembly will feel to be tighter. Not tighter like the joints do not move freely, more like the tightness you feel in a new car. Where the parts all move freely, but without the slack or looseness they get over years of use.

The Modified Hand And Arm Movements

Since the body does not pivot for these shorter shots we modify the arm actions by allowing them to swing from the shoulder sockets, Something we must not do in the longer shots. In these photos the shoulders elbows and wrists move in concert to swing the club from behind the point of the triangle to in front of it. **These arm actions can be used in play for all shots shorter than 3/8 shots.** For 3/8 and larger shots the left arm remains across the chest until after impact. **The weight must remain on the left foot, and must not move right.**

The photos above are blow ups of the hands in the photos in the top photos. The club has swung through the arc and the hands have released under. The hands will almost feel as if they are not moving at all, since the motion is not one of the hands but instead the wrist axles. Due to that the feel of the club twirling beneath the hands is slower than we may expect. The hands are part of the club, and move with the swing of the club beneath the wrist axles. Going back the right wrist flexes straight back and the left wrist gets a slight bow. Going through the left wrist flexes allowing the left palm to face down (you can't see it, but it is). The right wrist gets a bow as it tosses the clubhead past the point of the triangle. To allow the club to swing the left elbow relaxes and flexes. The flex and bow are not seen in these photos, but have happened. In the photo above left the right wrist has a large cup as does the left wrist in the photo above right. When the arms move from the shoulder sockets the bow of the left wrist nearly disappears visually, although a small amount must remain at the top of the back swing. **To release a bowed wrist, we must have some bow to release.**

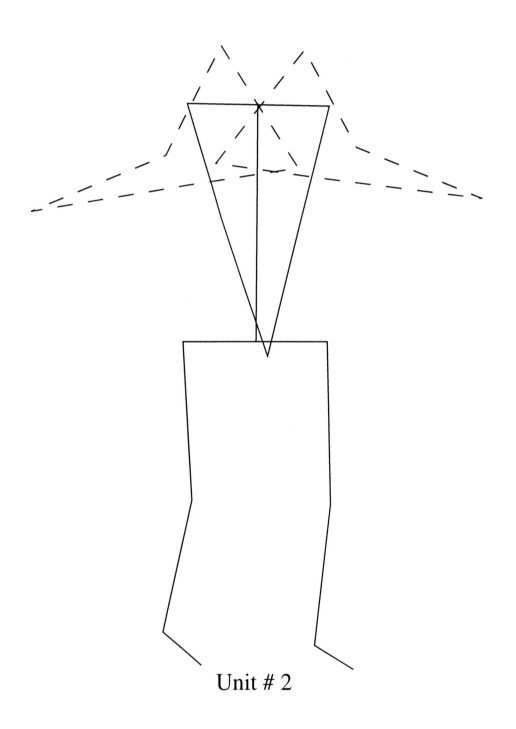

Unit # 2

UNIT # 2
The Triangle

THE FORMULA FOR POWER AND ACCURACY

Unit #2

The sketch on page 72, shows the body with the shoulders and the arms (solid lines). It also shows two additional triangles (dotted lines). Notice that each of the triangles has a bend in one of the sides, the base being the shoulder line with the bending occurring at the elbows. Since this is a static drawing, the body has not moved only the triangle. This is an illustration of how the arms fold, the body would move with this swing since the entire body is always involved on this much of a swing. Notice also in the sketch that the triangle rotates around a fixed point.

Swinging back the left arm (for right handed players) remains straight, and as can be seen from the photos below, the right elbow flexes <u>downward, as does the right upper arm from the shoulder.</u> The left arm does not raise up, instead it follows the turn of the body and slides up the chest in an arc (tight to the chest) as the left palm feels to seek the turning right shoulder. The right arm, which is relaxed, simply folds into the arc of the left arm. By folding this way the point of the triangle moves to the players right. The action of the right arm is very similar to those of a trombone players right arm. Later, when the pivot is added to this combination of arm movements and the wind-up of the forearms, the clubhead will swing on a single plane.

By not raising the arms from the shoulder sockets and simply turning the shoulders the clubhead remains on plane.

Since the body turns on a tilt, the arms swing up without raising them from the shoulder sockets.

In the photo above left Jaacob demonstrates the basic right arm fold in the standing up position, as you can see the left arm has swung up to shoulder height in an arc. The left arm is held tight to the chest. He does not lift the hands, or his right thumb vertically. The shortening of the right side of the triangle, as the right elbow and upper arm fold, happens naturally if the left hand pushes the left palm, toward the turning right shoulder, with no help from a relaxed right arm. As the arms swing to the right the arm pit opens and the right elbow swings away from the rib cage, as this happens the left hand due to the winding forearms gets above the right elbow. These actions are a natural result of the forearm wind up and the right shoulder blade adducting (text pg. 131).

The left arm must feel to be extended but not locked at the elbow. Once the left arm moves right of center on the larger shots (3/8 +) it remains there until after impact, we call this the # 7 position. The # 7 can plainly be seen in the right photo (white lines). The right arm however is active and straightens as it returns, not quite reaching straight at impact. It does reach straight soon after impact, and becomes a reverse #7 from there, as the left side of the triangle folds.

Shortening The Sides Of The Triangle

The triangle sides shorten and lengthen as the body rotates, this allows the point of the triangle to travel in a circular manner with a consistent radius. Since the club remains the same length and the circle of the hands revolves around a fixed point with one arm always extended the clubface returns to the ball correctly simply by straightening the shortened side. During the back swing the right arm collapses into the arc formed by the left arm. Swinging down it straightens naturally as we swing the club After impact the left side of the triangle collapses and the right arm becomes the radius as the relaxed left arm trombones.

These photos only show the beginning of the point of the triangles movement caused by the early actions of the wrists and elbows, as the sides of the triangle shorten the straight arm moves.

The solid line shows the 90 degree angle formed by the club shaft and the right forearm. The dotted lines show the original arm / shaft angle having not changed. Showing no vertical wrist cock.

Above left at address, the club is not centered on the triangle, it is in line with the left arm. Above right the right arm has tromboned, allowing the clubhead to retract 90 degrees behind the point of the triangle. Notice the 90 degree angle of the shaft and the right forearm, and the original downward angle of the left wrist axle. Our 90 degrees of wrist cock can be seen here, it occurs between the right forearm and club shaft, not the left arm and shaft as in the common swing.

Here we can see how the folding of the left elbow and the motions of the wrists as they release swing the club as the left side of the triangle begins to collapse .

When the elbows swing out as the upper arm bone lowers from the shoulder socket (facing page) we get the full movement of the triangles point. The after impact position is the exact mirror image.

As the club releases the left arm trombones allowing the right hand to hit through. Notice the 90 degree angle between the shaft and the left forearm. This shows that the clubhead has released the full 180 degrees around the wrist axles. These photos were posed to show the folding elbows, in an actual swing there would be much body action accompanying their actions and would be seen to happen in a different location in the swing. This arm / club position would be just after the right arm is parallel to the ground, and the body would be turned more.

Training the Elbows With The 1/4 Shot

Now that we know how the triangle sides shorten and lengthen we will continue building the swing. The next shot is to be learned once the elbow actions are understood and The Little Shot is working well. This shot is the 1/4 shot, it uses the hand actions of the little shot (page 48) but adds the actions of the elbows.

On the next pages you will be learning how to use these elbow actions, the motions seen need to be practiced every time you hit balls. At first work only on the Little Shot hand drills seen on the previous pages, after that shot is going well begin to work on the elbow drills for the 1/4 shot, as you also continue working on The Little Shot (1/8 shot).

The back swing of the 1/4 shot finds the butt end of the club shaft pointing at the target, the right elbow flexed and the hands moved only slightly to allow the right elbow to get alongside the right hip (the right elbow has not totally set in the photo above, the club would be at the dotted line). Notice the tucked left pinky knuckle (arrow). Notice, that although the clubhead goes straight back and up due to the pinky tuck, that the arc is bent to a tilted one as the right elbow folds.

The finish position is exactly the reverse of this one, as if a mirror image, except for the hand location on the shaft. Notice that the right hand is always closer to the clubhead arc than the left. The knees and feet never move in this shot, the weight stays left. Keeping the weight on the left heel guarantees crisp impact. Be sure to not shift any weight to the right foot. In this short of a shot there is not enough time for the weight to shift back to the left heel, where it must be at impact.

The Partial Shots

These shots train the right arm in the motion it makes in the lower section of the conical release. This shot is called the 1/4 shot since it produces roughly 1/4 of the distance of a full shot, and can be done with all clubs. If you hit your wedge 100 yards a properly done 1/4 shot will go 25 yards, more or less depending on the surface that it lands on. If you hit your 3 iron 200 yards, your 1/4 3 iron would go roughly 50 yards assuming similar surface conditions.

This gives you a good way of determining what club to hit, and how hard to hit it, when close to the green or trying to run a shot up from some distance. By dividing the shots from the 1/8 to the full by 1/8 ths we can arm ourselves with an arsenal of shots that allow different trajectories and roll out. The 1/4 shot positions are shown in the 2 photos below. This shot, and the others in its family 1/8 , 3/8, 1/2, 5/8 etc. will be easy to learn, and will prove invaluable in play.

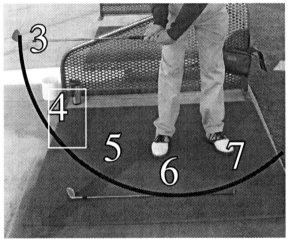

Both of the above photos were taken without Jim having moved. Notice that the club shaft is both parallel to the ground and also to the line of flight, you cannot see it from these pix, but the shaft is also parallel to and directly beneath the shoulders. The exact motions of the hands from the 1/8 shot, as the wrists set, were used. When the elbow gets involved, and the right arm folds, the clubface arc is bent inward. The club swings up and in as the hands and elbow work to this position. The left wrist works as the pin in the center of a clock face tilted at the shaft angle. Notice that the clubhead has moved from 6 to 3. Naturally going down the clubhead would swing from 3 to 6 and then up to 9. Swing down and through gently, make sure that the right hand passes between the left hand and the ball, and that the left wrist axle releases as it must in all full golf shots.

That entire motion is the 1/4 swing. Again I must stress there is no leg action or chest turn. 98% of the weight is on and stays on the left foot. The only weight on the right foot for this entire motion is the weight of the right foot itself.

The Tromboning Of The Arms

To correctly swing the club, the sides of triangle shorten by "tromboning" the right and then the left arm. See the sketch at the start of the chapter (page 72) and the photo facing page. The reason we give it this special name is that the action is similar to the arm action a slide trombone player would make, if he pulled in the slide as he swung the horn to his right. It must be accompanied by the forearm wind up, and the upper arm (humerus) bone rotating to the right from inside the shoulder socket. These actions open the right armpit, positioning the triangles lever assembly correctly (facing page).

This action gets the clubhead, and right hand as far away as possible from the ball, so that we will have more space and time to accelerate it, on its way back to the ball. The sequence is more than the simple bending of the elbow and it accomplishes two objectives. By tromboning the right arm, while winding the forearms (facing page), it shortens the right side of the arm-shoulder triangle and keeps the clubhead on the perfect plane. The position the right arm attains at the top of the back swing can be seen in the top left photo on page 146. This action greatly simplifies the return arc, since it simply reverses coming down.

Going back, push the club back with the left palm across the chest in a conical arc from the left shoulder, under and up. Feel the left arm slide slightly up the chest as the left palm seeks the turning right shoulder. As you start slightly tuck under the left pinky knuckle with a slight counter-clockwise twist of the shaft, and fold the right wrist hinge, the right knuckles will feel to lead the right hand back.

The relaxing right elbow must fold in a curling manner, **without influencing the left arms actions**. As this happens the right forearm winds up in a **counter-clockwise** manner. Swinging down, the right arm operates by un-tromboning exactly opposite of the way it went back. It twirls the club as it extends and throws through to complete the release.

Due to its correct winding up actions the return will be guided by simply doing the opposite movements and it will return perfectly if we let it. The right hand will toss through under the left wrist axle and the arms will reverse their roles. The straight right arm seeks the turning left shoulder as the left arm trombones.

On both sides of the swing the tromboning arm will position its hand in "The Cop Saying Stop" position. See photos page 147.

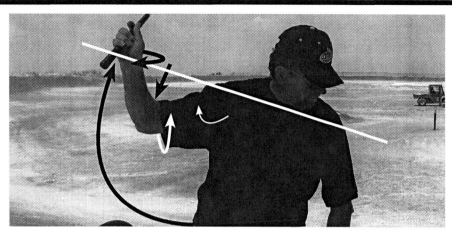

This photo shows the 4 movements of the tromboning right arm action. The right upper arm has rotated to the right from within the shoulder socket (small white arrow at shoulder). This causes the entire arm to travel to the right in the direction of the black arrow by the palm. As this happens the upper arm is folding down and in (small black arrow), shortening the arm. The right arm folds into the arc of the left arm as the left arm swings up across the chest seeking the turning right shoulder. The right hand ends up directly over the right elbow, but does not lift to get there. Instead the humerus lowers from the shoulder socket as the right upper arm above the elbow rotates (curved white arrow at elbow). These arm actions maintain the clubhead in a single plane.

The right forearm winds in the direction of the curved arrow at the wrist, as it does the hand travels to where the left arm pushes it, depicted by the white line across the shoulders   . Using only one hand start from the position shown in the top left photo on page 146, and unwind the forearm as you turn through and swing the club, you will begin to feel just how powerfully you can use the right arm from there. The upper bone in the right arm must not pull, it will travel with the chest and stay alongside the chest as the chest turns in a position similar to its position in the photo above. If Jaacob were to turn the chest left by using his legs the right arm would rotate as well. Moving the right upper arm forward independently would only use the chest muscles rather than the legs. It would be nowhere near as powerful and much harder to control.

The right forearm has not wound up in the above photo, only rotated to illustrate the position attained by the turn of the upper right arm. When the forearms, and the upper arm bone complete their wind up the palm will face the sky and the forearm would be turned a few degrees more. The arrows show the directions of their rotation, the section on the wind-up of the forearms will explain these actions in detail. The finished arm movement is hard to spot to the untrained eye. It, like the entire rest of the body's movements, will appear to just be a beautiful, effortless and powerful golf swing. Exactly what is being done is invisible to a viewer not knowing the details of this swing.

Maintaining The Arc

The arc of the golf swing must remain as large as possible to generate the power needed for quality golf shots. To maintain this large arc the right thumb must stay down, and the slight bow at the back of the left wrist must be maintained. The photos below will show and explain why.

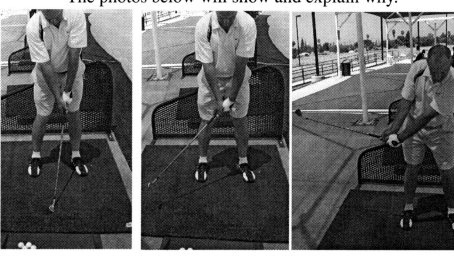

Above left Gary Sanati is at address, in the center photo he has counter-rotated the club by twisting the shaft as the right wrist set the club to a position 45 degrees right of the point of the triangle, this is our version of wrist cock. Although technically a part of Unit #3 the shoulder turn is shown here. From here he simply keeps his thumb down and continues the forearm wind up to the top of the back swing. This keeps the arc broad and forces a good full shoulder turn.

Notice that he never lets the small bow of the left wrist break down, doing this puts the left wrist into a position that does not allow vertical wrist cock. Try this yourself, bow your left wrist (empty handed) now try to move your hand in a hitch hike vertical movement from the wrist. You will find that it does not cock vertically very much. In this swing it does not need to, nor do we want it to. Our wrist cock is sideways (as in top center photo) not vertical.

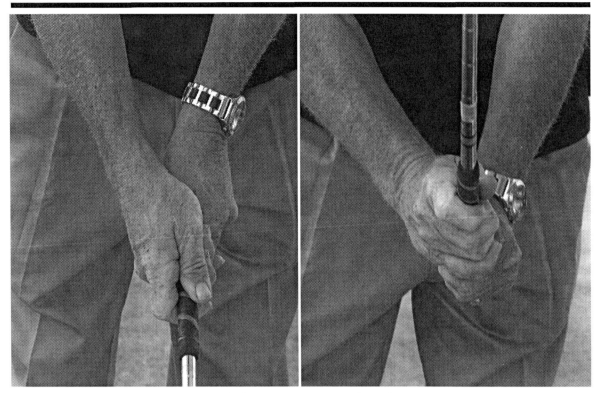

When the left wrist has a cup it is easy to cock the club up, since from the cupped wrist position the hand itself moves in that direction easily.

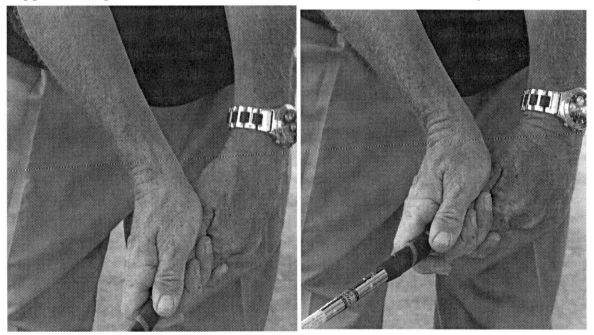

If you bow the left wrist, it creates a stop and does not allow the lift of the club more than a few degrees, this maintains a large clubhead arc for more power and better impact. Try it yourself, you will see that the slightly bowed wrist does not raise much. By doing this we can make the circle that the clubhead travels in much larger, in effect we will be hitting the ball with a longer lever.

THE FORMULA FOR POWER AND ACCURACY

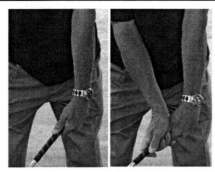

If the point of the triangle does not move both wrists would have an equal amount of movement and bow. This teaches the movements of the axles.

Use a mirror to view this picture in reverse to see elbow flex and the rotation of the left forearm after impact. This action gets the left arm out of the way.

When the elbow flexes, the arm with the downward bent elbow will have a large flex at the wrist, but the movement of the point of the triangle sideways will cause the other wrist to lose the look of the bow. This can plainly be seen in the photo above, the right arm and shaft get a 90 degree angle, illustrated by the white lines. The left arm and shaft keep the arm shaft angle set at address and only move the clubhead to the right of the point of the triangle (dashed lines). The point of the triangle also moves sideways slightly reducing the slight left wrist bow yet maintaining the large right wrist cock, as can be seen above. The left wrist must still have a little bow to properly release. The bow keeps the thumbs from rising, as it keeps the clubhead on plane, it keeps the arc broad. The combined wrist, elbow, upper arm and shoulder motions keep the face aligned, and the clubhead under control. It is plain to see the power that can be added to the clubhead with the right arm from this position. Beyond this point in the back swing, the right forearm winds up in the direction of the white curved arrow, this swings the right elbow out to the perfect throwing position. At the top of the back swing the hands will still be in the exact position that they occupy in the top right and lower photo.

Hitting is done with the straightening of the right arm combined with the reverse of the forearm wind up and the wrist axle toss hand movements. After impact the fore-arm unwind continues, swinging the left humerus up and out of the way as the left elbow trombones down. Beyond the hit the left forearm must rotate in the opposite direction of the rotation of the white arrow. A mirror will let you view it in reverse.

How, But Not When, The Arms Swing From
The Shoulder Sockets

When the wrist axles and elbows are used correctly the point of the triangle moves from centered, to a position right of center (exactly where depends on body type), and going through swings to a position left of center. For this to happen the arms must swing in an arc below the shoulders. Beyond these positions the palm of the straight arm seeks the turning shoulder of the flexed arm.

Where, When And How, The Arms Swing
From The Shoulder Sockets

This swinging from the shoulder actions does not occur as shown in the top photos except in shots up to 1/4 shots. **From the 3/8 shot on the swing from the shoulders occurs after impact.** The left arm remains back across the chest, however the right arm is very active in a twirling and throwing type action. In the photo above (lower left) the left arm has been driven all of the way to the impact position by the pivot. In the photo to the right the hips are almost exactly where they were just before impact, they did not stop turning. The triangle re-formed momentarily, and then the left side collapsed. The right arm is now fully released and is in the reverse of the #7 position. It is tight to the right pectoral muscle, and will remain there until the end of the swing.

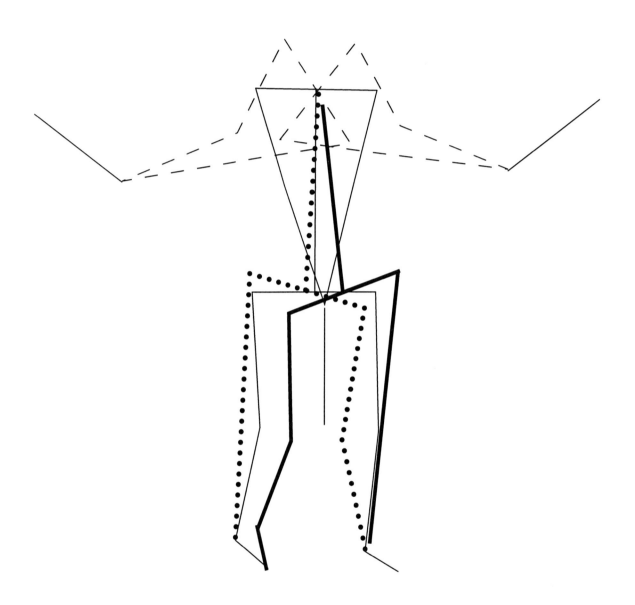

Units 1, 2 and 3

UNIT # 3
The Actions of The Body

The Reason For The Pivot

In golf you can't be very accurate running up to the ball as Happy Gilmore did in the movie of the same name, due to the inconsistent location of the swing circle center, but you can in fact retreat as far as possible behind our ball. As a matter of fact any movement of the swing circle center breeds inaccuracy, although some very talented players have through repetition played good golf despite having it.

The object of the back swing is to remove all of the slack in the mechanism, and get the clubhead far away from our left heel. Done correctly all of our levers get set in a powerful and controlled position. By doing this we gain space and time to hit the golf ball by using all the levers of the swing for the hitting action. We do this by shifting our weight, while maintaining our balance, and turning behind the ball while keeping our swing circle center fixed in space.

Doing this eliminates any slack in the connection between the left heel and the clubhead. It is the elimination of slack that allows us to swing from the ground up, and at the same time from the top down, without losing the pull that the left side of the body produces as the weight shifts back to the left leg. Once the slack is removed from the mechanism, it must not come back. The chest must remain to the right of the hips as the legs shift the weight and drive the left arm around with the pivot. For a more graphic mental picture of keeping the slack out see the sketches and captions on page 96.

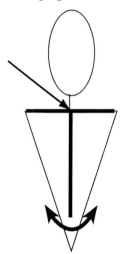

As the body shifts the weight the bottom of the "T" created by the spine and shoulders moves from side to side. By so doing it tilts the shoulders around the point of the arrow. This action moves the weight from a 2 foot balance to a one foot balance, and gets us behind the ball.

As we return through the ball, this shifting of the lower end of the spine repositions the angle of the spine. This both provides power by driving the triangles left arm and creates the proper path for the swing of the club. In so doing it also provides a stable swing circle center.

The swing circle center is the point in space that anchors and locates the center of the arc of the clubheads travel. If it moves it must be returned to the same place, relative to the ball, for solid clubhead / ball contact. Any location other than this will diminish solid contact as well as clubhead speed. Since that is the case the "T" must rock to keep it still, while still creating much power.

Unit #3 The Body

The body actions of this swing, in the pivot, create a compound lever action. It uses the body weight and the actions of the legs to move the spine first as a lever and later as a drive shaft. A compound leveraged action is much more powerful than a simple lever, using the actions of the feet, knees and hips to first tilt, and then turn the chest. By doing these things correctly the feet, knees and hips control the directions of, and add power to, Units #1 and 2.

The body is supported by the legs which are mounted on the outboard ends of the pelvis. Due to that design feature, to move the mass of the body's weight behind the ball without moving the top end of the spine the lower end of the spine must move. If the player tries to keep the lower end of the spine still, by attempting to hold the lower body still and only turning the top to wind up the torso, the head will move and with it moves the swing circle center. When the swing circle center moves, impact then becomes uncertain. Head movement starts from the concept of winding the body to create torque, which the player would then use by unwinding the trunk muscles. This causes much strain to the back.

Using the following coordinated actions of the feet, knees and hip tilt causes the lower end of the spine to move. First make a post of the right leg for the body to turn on in the back swing. Then reverse those actions going through and make a post of the left leg swinging through. By using the legs as posts it creates a stable platform on which the actions of the other leg turns the hips. Another benefit is, one leg or the other will always be straight while the opposite leg bends, thus the head will not move up and down. This creates more stability while allowing full use of the movements and thus the power of the legs. With this pivot the swing circle center remains still and anchors the center of the clubheads arc with precision.

To use the legs in their most efficient manner requires the correct use of the feet, knees and hips as well. The actions used are practiced daily in the act of walking. When walking the weight shifts from one foot to the other as the knees move back and forth and the heels move up and down. These exact same actions occur as we pivot, but with an additional lateral movement of the hips. These actions are similar to the natural walking actions of a woman. The lower end of the spine will visibly move left and right as the weight shifts. This creates a very stable head and swing circle center and allows the body the freedom to move beneath it.

The next 6 pages show sketches and photos with captions that will detail both the concept of the hip, knee and spine actions as well as creating a mental image of what the skeleton is doing as you view the picture series.

THE FORMULA FOR POWER AND ACCURACY

Leverage

The energy we send into the golf ball comes from the speed of the clubhead as we swing. This energy comes from the electrical energy our brain sends to stimulate muscular activity which then causes the muscles to move the framework of the body. The body will be used as a system of levers, and the following sketch series will show what each lever does and how they work as a unit.

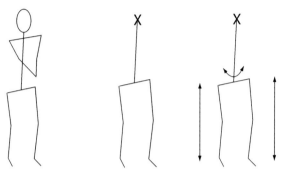

In the sketches above, is a stick figure of the whole lever assembly. The center one has no head or arms and an X showing the only stationary part of the entire lever assembly, the swing circle center, it acts both as a fulcrum and a locator for the top of the triangle as it rotates. The sketch below right, shows the motion of the lower end of the spine as the belly button slides right and left. The vertical arrows show the direction of motion of the hips as they tilt and turn due to the actions of the ankles and knees. As one knee straightens the other bends, this sliding laterally motion of the pelvis keeps the swing circle center still.

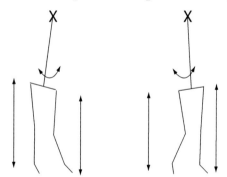

The sketch above left shows the right knee retracted to straight, and the left knee flexed and pointing at the ball. Notice that the hips have rotated 45 degrees right just from this action, there has been no attempt to turn the hips or the chest, the pelvis has slid right so that the lower end of the spine is pointing directly at the right heel. The sketch above right shows the return hip slide caused by the opposite knee and ankle motions. The hips have rotated the opposite way, and now are 45 degrees left of the address position. The simple act of straightening one knee and flexing the other as the hips slide right and left turns the hips 90 degrees. This is a very important point since it is the amount of chest turn needed to square the chest at impact from the position it will be in at the top of the back swing.

The sketch below is the same sketch as the one at the lower left of the previous page, the box that has been added represents the chest. Here we see the chest rotated an additional 45 degrees beyond where the hips were moved by the feet and knees. The chest is now 90 degrees to the flight line, the back is to the target.

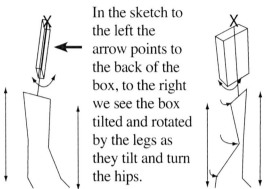

In the sketch to the left the arrow points to the back of the box, to the right we see the box tilted and rotated by the legs as they tilt and turn the hips.

Notice throughout this sketch series that the knees are moving only in a hinge like manner, the weight is shifting from one foot to the other as the knees straighten and flex and the hips slide. Thus the straightening left leg drives the left shoulder up, and levers the left arm down around the fulcrum of the 7th cervical.

Since we know that simply moving the knees and feet while laterally sliding the hips rotates the hips 90 degrees, If the player makes no attempt to turn either the hips or the chest the actions of the feet and knees will rotate the chest square with (parallel to) the flight line. As the right heel turns out the rotation of the hips turn it through. Since the body is not consciously turning, the left arm path will feel to be 45 degrees across the flight line from in to out. The sideward leveraged movement becomes rotational as the right heel continues to rise and turn out toward the flight line. This action changes the lateral slide into a rotation as the right leg runs around the posted left leg and rotates the hips. This hip rotation occurs as the clubhead is passing through impact, the hips turn the chest, powering the left arm. The rotating hips drive the chest around bringing Unit #2 as both Units # 1 & 2 operate. The downswing path of the left hand is thus controlled by hip slide. The rotation of the hips bends the cross line path to a circular arc around and up over the left shoulder. The left arm is driven straight down the flight line by the turning hips and chest during impact, with the hands and clubhead arriving at the ball with the right knee.

Try this for yourself, standing erect and with both knees slightly flexed, pull the right knee (not the hip) back until it is straight, as you do this flex your left knee and let your belly button slide directly right. You should arrive at a position of being on your right foot and having your left knee directly under your chin. If you did it right your hips and chest are now turned 45 degrees. These are the correct actions of the skeletal frame, as you make the proper back swing weight shift, reversing returns it.

THE FORMULA FOR POWER AND ACCURACY

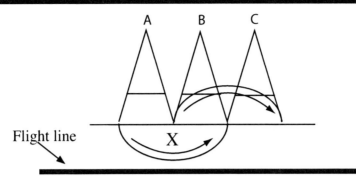

In mechanical drawing you divide the length of a line by using a compass or dividers to mark off divisions. Starting from the left the compass swings an arc on the leg at point X, when done it assumes the position of the compass at B. Continuing the movement, the next pivot (behind the line) gets the compass to position C. This illustrates a toward and away from the line concept. In our pivot we never pivot away from the flight line only in toward it as does the pivot in the sketch below.

Here are 2 pair of dividers each pivoting toward the flight line on the center stationary leg. Turning this way both creates the stable head position, and **turns the body behind the ball, not away from the flight line**. The top point of each pair of dividers represents the ball socket of the hip where it attaches to the pelvis.

The above sketches do not take into account the actions of the ankle joints, the photo series will deal with their exact movements. The larger arrows are the hips, and the small arrows depict knee movements. Notice that the hips turn in toward the ball not away from it. The right knee retracts to straight, creating a post. **Do not attempt to pull back or turn the right hip**. Instead simply straighten the leg by pulling the right knee back to straight. Done correctly the leg will be straight and vertical, and the pelvis will have turned in toward the flight line on the post. The return pivot is a simple reversing of the above actions. Pivoting this way creates much power while feeling effortless, since it creates a position of balance that naturally requires the correct return actions to maintain balance. The leg action will be simple to learn and do, but it must be practiced and done exactly for a long enough period to overcome your history.

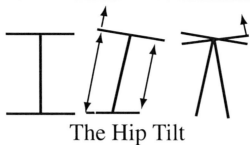

The Hip Tilt

The leg action that tilts the "T" in the weight shift, works in concert with the muscles within the torso that tilt the hips. These muscles are very powerful, and their use provides the lever action of the spine, adding much power to the golf swing. To tilt the hips simply pull the lower left rib close to the left hip bone as you swing back and reverse that action by pulling the right side of the rib cage close to the right hip coming down (see photos on pages 148,149 and 150). The tilt of the hips moves the body weight laterally from one leg to the other. The posting and running actions of the legs then combine with the hip tilt to drive the rotating torso through the pivot. Used together they cause and power the weight shift and when swinging back down create a powerful pivot. The weight shift and pivot will not happen correctly without the correct tilt of the hips.

The sketch, above left, shows a large letter "I" the top bar of the I represents the shoulders, the vertical bar the spine and the lower bar the pelvis. This gives a good starting point for learning how the hip tilt works. The sketch, above right, shows the shoulders and spine as a large letter "T". The sketch shows the tilt of the spine and rock of the shoulders. The movements of the torso are this, the upper bar and the vertical bar do not ever change their relationship. They remain in the "T" position throughout the entire swing, the "T" never becomes mis-shapen as in "*T*". In other words when the "T" tilts around the spot where the upper bar and the vertical bar intersect, the 90 degree angles remain 90 degrees. Any sideways movement of the lower end of the spine thus causes the top bar to tilt.

The lower bar of the "I". The pelvis does tilt relative to the spine by the use of the muscles within the torso. This action is very important to understand since tilting the pelvis this way causes the lower end of the spine to move as it slides to the post of the right leg. The right side of the body becomes long from the shoulder to the ground, as the left side becomes short. The left shoulder gets closer to the left hip as the left knee flexes. When we do this we can turn the left side of the torso from the hip to the shoulders between the spine and the ball, around a fixed point (the intersection of the "T"), thus keeping a very still swing circle center. Reversing the above actions returns the pivot and allows the entire right side of the body to rotate between the spine and the ball as we hit through the shot. The correct tilt and re-tilt of the hips helps create the perfect pivot.

The Hip Turn

To maintain a stable swing circle center the body must turn beneath it as the legs do their part to hold up the body while supplying a strong rotational force to the shoulder / arm package. The legs in concert with the internal trunk muscles that slightly tilt the hips do this by transferring the weight from its starting position of equally on both feet, and also equally across the soles of both feet, to a one foot balance with the weight that was on the left heel feeling to roll over to the ball of the left foot. Since we set up behind the ball we do not need to go there, thus the head and swing-circle-center must not move right.

Swinging back down, first the spine and pelvis slide laterally left as the hips fully re-tilt, causing the body to get to a one foot balance on the left foot. Once the shift is complete; the hips due to the right leg action and the turn out of the right heel, turn the chest through the ball, with the right foot ending up with what's left (very little) of the body weight on the very tip of the right big toe.

For this to happen the lower end of the spine must be allowed to slide a small amount right, (for a right handed player) as the player makes his turn away from the ball. The lower end of the spine makes a small conical action in toward the flight line and a small slide laterally right. Completed the spine will feel to point directly at the right heel. To do this yet keep the swing circle center from moving, the right leg must maintain its position. **Without retracting** the right hip slides a small amount laterally to the right. As the hips slide to the right the left heel slightly rises and the left knee flexes and rotates in to point a little behind the ball. This is done without the right hip going away from the flight line. This action turns the left hip in towards the ball. By turning the left hip in and rotating the body on the top of the right leg without allowing the right hip to retract we wind up the muscles of the upper right leg and get the weight turned behind the ball and not away from the ball.

For all of those above actions to function correctly the left side, front and rear internal trunk muscles, must shorten and feel to pull the left lower rib toward the left hip bone, the feeling is as if we were lifting the hip. This action helps slide the spine laterally a little to point roughly at the right heel and controls the hip turn. The above action lowers the left shoulder creating the beginning of the arm swing away from the ball. Once tilted the shoulders rotate and by doing so wind up the tilted trunk. The picture series and captions on the following pages will both show and explain these things in a simple to understand manner.

The Axle Of The Spine And Its Use As A Lever

The spine has several functions in this golf swing, it acts as a drive shaft to turn the arm / shoulder triangle through the shot as it rotates. It also functions both as an axle to locate the rotating shoulders, and a lever. The movement of the bottom of this lever creates the early motion of the shoulders. The lateral hip slide controls the path of the left hand, and by doing so it also controls the correct plane of the clubhead and its path. It does this first with leverage as the lower end of the spine slides laterally over from a one foot balance on the right foot to create a one legged balance on the forward post (left leg). As the shift nears its completion, the right leg runs around the posted left leg, this action rotates the hips. By doing so they bring with them the chest and the left arm which remains in the #7 position. **The shift forward to the left leg re-tilts the "T" causing the arms to swing up as the clubhead swings down, the beginning of this can be seen in the right photo below.** The right arm makes the twirling clubhead catch-up to and pass the left wrist. The free swinging pendulum (golf club) releases massive energy into the ball, as long as the left wrist hinges freely. If the wrist locks up due to a death grip, or locked wrist axle, the club does not swing freely and power as well as accuracy is sacrificed.

In the 2 photos above we can observe the weight shift that returns the left arm all of the way to the ball. The body has made no attempt to turn, but since the knees have reversed their actions and the hips have shifted laterally, the "T" has re-tilted. The hips have turned 90 degrees, this has squared the chest to the flight line. From this point onward the left arm is driven by the right leg as the right heel turns out toward the flight line. The turning out of the heel rotates the hips and with them the axle of the spine which then rotates the chest, arms and of course the returning clubhead. The feel of this action is of stepping from the right foot to the left foot as the right side lower back muscles pull the right shoulder into the right hip pocket. The back feels to arch. <u>The belly should feel to go up under the left arm.</u> Done in this fashion the legs, by shifting the weight, leverage the left arm downward around the fulcrum of the swing circle center to the position seen above right. The leveraged action then blends into a rotation as the pelvis rotates on the posted left leg. Thus the legs and hip tilt, by moving the bottom end of the "T" and then rotating it, provide massive power to the left arm. The entire sequence of GJ's swing is on pages 34 and 35.

THE FORMULA FOR POWER AND ACCURACY

How The Pivot Swings Units #1 and #2

The arms must be swung by the pivot, they must not swing independently of the body. In other words the spokes of the wheel rotate at the same speed as the axle. However the right arm, while staying back is active. When you reverse its back swing actions it straightens and makes the club catch the left arm, the faster the left arm moves and the faster the club catches it the farther the ball goes.

Later on when hitting fuller shots refer to all of the photos throughout the book

The left arm does not swing from the shoulder blades until after the ball is struck, it must remain in the #7 position across the chest and act like a spoke turning with the axle of the spine (photos above). The right arm however is active, and swings from the shoulder socket in a throwing manner (photos below).

As the downswing starts the forearms begin to unwind, this action frees up the right triceps muscle which then straightens the right arm. The right upper arm bone rotates around due to this action. Appearing to return close to the right hip. The right elbow close to the hip position is not attained by pulling down the elbow toward the hip, it is caused by the shortening of the right side of the body and the lengthening of the left side by the correct use of Unit #3. The right elbow and upper arm are actually rising as the arm straightens. Refer to the 2 lower photos as you work on the 3/8 and 1/2 shots, soon to be learned.

Maintaining The Wind Up Of The Body

To get the full use of the actions of the body, the pivot starts the motion from the ground up, exactly as the right hand and arm start the clubhead around the back side of the downswing arc to make it catch up to the left hand. Both of these actions happen together and must be timed to happen so that the explosion of impact happens in the right place relative to the body. The impact does not occur in front of the body, it happens alongside of or (depending on your body's limitations) slightly in front of the right hip, just as the right hip is being turned into the ball by the outward rotation of the right heel.

For this to happen, the start down from the top of the back swing must be slow and the wound up condition of the body from the left heel to the clubhead must be maintained. Every body part turned right must feel to stay right except for Unit #3 as it returns the triangle. The only exception to that is the right arm, it must be very active to make the clubhead catch up to, and pass, the hands. The angles of the triangle must return and re-form the triangle.

The simple act of replanting the left heel and picking up the right heel as we shorten the right side of the body slides the hips left and begins the rotation to the wound up body as it levers the left arm all of the way down until just before impact. At the wrist axles swing the club the right heel must rotate out toward the flight line to keep the left arm moving, if it does not the shot will be pushed right and have less power. The timing of this will be a natural action and should not be hard to time in the full swing if grooved in the shorter swings, and the start down is slow.

The left shoulder absolutely must be in the fully wound condition attained at the top, the left arm #7 position must be maintained until after impact and the right arm must twirl and throw the clubhead around the point of the approaching triangle timed to hit the ball as the left arm and club almost, but not quite, reach the in line condition we had at address. It straightens very shortly after the ball is gone. The back of the left hand must be facing the target, as the right hand passes through, the ball then has no choice but to fly straight, high and true.

These are the components of a golf swing that is as mechanically as accurate and powerful a movement as the mechanism of the human body can attain. This swing conforms to the body's design and will cause the least strain upon it. It can be used for a lifetime of good golf, and will work for the young as well as those with more experienced bodies. Reasonably fit seniors will find this swing a blessing, since it is very powerful and yet very easy on the body.

Towing A Car

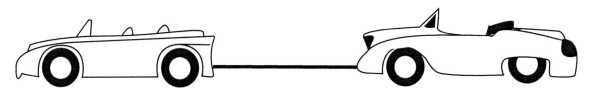

In the above sketch we have a car towing another, since the rope is taut (no slack) when the front car moves forward so does the rear car. If they should have to stop the driver of the rear car would do all of the braking and the rope would stay taut for the next start up. If the driver of the rear car does not apply his brakes to stop the front car the rope becomes slack and the front car cannot pull the rear car until the rope is again taut. If slack occurs the power of the front car does not get to the rear car.

There would be a big bump and the rope may break.

So it is in the golf swing. The power, that rotates the triangle, comes from the ground up. When the body begins to return the clubhead to the ball all slack must be out if we are to efficiently apply the bodies power to the ball. If the body unwinds and the shoulders catch up to the hips, or if the left shoulder and arm swings away from the chest instead of remaining in the, # 7, across the chest position much of the drive of the weight shift and pivot are lost.

For the body to use the strength of the legs efficiently the slack must be removed from the clubhead all of the way to the left heel during the back swing. The slack must not be allowed to return. The chest must remain tightly wound to the right of the hips and the left upper arm pinned to the chest.

The weight shift and turn then drive the triangle directly. This is not possible if the arms move forward around the body rather than returning with the chest, at the same speed as the turn, and not faster than it. The spokes of a wheel cannot travel faster than the axle. The axle is driven from the bottom end. The legs are the motor of the golf swing and supply most of the power, but they can only do it if the wind up is maintained.

To maintain the wind up of the body, the ball must be struck off the side of the right hip, not in front of the body. If struck in front of the body the wind up is lost. Just as in towing a car the front car cannot zoom away; the rope would break when towing the car and the back car would be disconnected from the power source. In the golf swing we may also lose the connection, since unwanted torso unwind can easily happen, also the start down may not be in the right direction. It is critical to start the down swing correctly, the initial movement down must be slow and controlled to keep the rotation on the proper plane.

The first few feet of the return of the triangle determines the path of the entire swing. If we go wrong in these first 2 feet, and the left hand is moved closer to the flight line by a turning action rather than traveling straight at the ball caused by the leveraged shift it is impossible to recover. Just as in firing a rifle, if the barrel is moved during the time that the bullet is travelling down it the shot will not hit the target. It is essential to accuracy to return the triangle down the correct delivery path. This is easily done if the start down to the ball is controlled by the shift forward of the spine during the phase of the down swing where it is acting like a lever.

It is equally easy to mis-direct the initial down swing rotation of the triangle by beginning to turn during the time that we are shifting. The shift must happen first, followed by the turn. To keep these things in the correct order it is essential to start the down swing slowly, the lateral movement of the hips and the movements of the feet and knees cannot be perfectly controlled as we are learning them if maximum speed is employed. The slower start down, plus a slightly smaller and less violent lateral shift is the basic difference between this swing and the long driving contest swing.

At first moving slowly laterally to start the down swing will give the feeling that we cannot strike the ball with much force. You will find that the opposite is true. There is plenty of time to get the clubhead up to speed, and the timing of getting the club back in the fully extended position will be much easier to accomplish. It will also feel much easier to stay behind the ball, and the feel of the hitting through releasing action will be easy to obtain. All of my long driving champions had to learn to slow down the start down to train the body to control the plane with the shift, only after much practice to groove this motion were these players able to swing full out and still have precision. Once learned this can be done during play, but good judgement must be used as to when it will give an advantage. In play where score is important and maximum distance is not, **less** distance and on the fairway, is usually **more**.

THE FORMULA FOR POWER AND ACCURACY

The Actions Of The Feet And Knees

The pivot of the body is mostly a product of the movements of the feet and the knees, the hips and internal torso muscles assist of course, but their actions are not possible without the leg action created by the correct use of the feet and knees.

To slide the lower end of the spine right and left the knees and feet must allow it, and the internal trunk muscles must assist it. The supporting leg (the right leg for righties) must be straightened by retraction of the knee, not the hip, this creates the post for the body to pivot on. As this happens the left knee must flex and the left heel must slightly rise as the weight shifts to the right foot, without intentionally lifting the heel. This action frees up the left knee to also rotate in and slide to the right, ending up directly below the chin. Done correctly it feels as if there is a wheel mounted directly below the left knee that rolls out and around to hold you up. The weight on the left foot will feel to roll over on to the inside of the ball of the left foot and the big toe. This action adds fore and aft support and balance. The photo series of the leg actions will show this graphically. The actions are similar to walking, one heel down, one heel up, as the hips slide side to side. No attempt should be made to turn the hips, the knee and foot actions alone take care of the hip turn.

When the knees and feet work as described they create and allow the weight shift and pivot. When they do not, the pivot cannot be done properly. Power will suffer, as will the lower back sooner or later. Retracting the right knee creates a straight and vertical post for the pelvis to turn in toward the ball on, this allows the left hip to turn in toward the flight line, turning our body behind the ball rather than away from it. Done this way the body will turn easily and in balance.

As we return and swing back to the impact area, the spine must slide over on to the top of the straight and vertically posted left leg before the body can turn on that post. The correct series of actions is a shift of weight and then a turn swinging back, and then a shift of weight followed by a turn coming through. When the pivot is done as described we get balance, power and the timing of the hit becomes much easier to do. The entire right side of the body can then hit through. The pivot, done this way, actually speeds up the rotation of the upper lever assembly. The arms and hands will have more time to get the clubhead up to speed and the body will feel to stay behind the ball. We can then swing the clubhead through the ball, rather than at the ball.

Here is the basic starting point for all golf shots, the width of the feet is quite narrow and does not widen much even on the longest of drives. The weight is evenly distributed between both feet and also evenly between the heel and toes. Notice that a slightly flexed right knee and extended right knee has caused the hips to rotate a few degrees open yet the chest remains square to the flight line. The chest is square to the flight line and the hips are already open to the chest, they will remain ahead of the chest until well after impact.

Notice also that the left leg is very nearly straight and, due only to the knee positions, that the bottom of the "T" representing the spine and shoulders is pointing almost at the left heel. Due to this small amount of knee flex and extension the top bar of the "T" has the right side (shoulder) lower than the left. This knee, hip and leg position slightly tilts the triangle and will allow the right hand to grasp the club with the left arm straight and the right only slightly flexed.

The back is straight and the weight is evenly distributed, for balance, fore and aft. The position should feel extremely comfortable, it should also feel very athletic. You should feel balanced and ready to move. The weight should be equal on both feet and evenly spread heel to toe.

In the photo above, and the one on the facing page, is the position you should attain simply by extending the left knee and retracting the right knee to straight.

No part of the body should be attempting to turn, this action is quite natural and no attempt to turn the hips is necessary, simply move the knees and allow the hips to slide right. Notice that the long line representing the spine now points at the right heel, this is the end of the hip movement. Hold them here. Now it is only necessary to rotate the left shoulder under the chin, this action is best done by pushing with the entire left side, the left arm, shoulder, hand and hip. As the left side pushes the right shoulder blade must adduct, which it does naturally when the forearms wind. The above pivot movements wind the torso and remove all slack in the body. The forearm wind removes all slack from Units #1 and 2. As the left heel starts down, the clubhead is immediately influenced. Notice, in both photos, that the top bar of the "T" remains a "T".

Notice in both photos how the left ankle everts* as the belly button moves right. Here we see how the left knee rotates and slides directly under the chin, it will then give fore and aft stability and the body will be as stable as a tripod.

*Ankle eversion is a rolling over of the foot to its inside edge as the heel lifts.

As the down swing begins it is essential that the hips do not feel to rotate, they must instead slide laterally. If the hips try to turn they over turn the chest, since it is fully wound to the right of the hips. This action causes the downswing to go out and around rather than bringing the arms down the correct inside path. The shot will then be pulled to the left and a perfect feeling swing will create a well struck ball that ends up missing the intended target to the left. It is very important to understand that the weight must shift fully on to the left leg before the hips turn, and that the turning of the hips, chest and Unit #2 be left to the feet and knee actions. The spine must move like a pendulum hung from the swing circle center, and once slid left it is then turned by the outward rotation of the right heel (toward the flight line), and the running like action of the right leg. By correctly first shifting the weight and sliding the hips, while the chest stays still, the resulting re-tilt of the spine, re-tilts the shoulders and keeps the correct in to out swing path controlled. Done correctly the downward tilt of the tip of the triangles orbit in the downswing is established, this eliminates the out and around action which causes the shots to be well struck but pulled. The correctly tilted spine, as the hips slide sideways, controls the tilt of the plane. The arms swing like spokes around the spine with their rise and fall controlled by the movement of the lower end of the tilting and rotating axle (the spine).

The hips must never attempt to rotate left, they simply slide laterally left to get the weight on to the left post. The turn of the body comes from the action of the right knee and the outward turn of the right heel, this action turns the hips which then in turn rotate the chest and shoulders. Both heels must work exactly together, if the left heel slams down before the right rises the hips turn prematurely and cause the above described pull. The sequence is shift and then turn. Set up a posted left leg by replanting the left heel, picking up the right heel and pulling the left knee (not the left hip) back to straight. Once on the posted leg, the right knee runs around the left leg, due to the lift and turn out of the right heel. This action delays the hip turn and makes them turn very quickly when they rotate.

In the photo above, Jim has made no attempt to turn, he has simply pulled the right knee in the direction of the arrow until it is straight. As he did this he also flexed the left knee and used the muscles on the inside of the upper left leg to pull the knee to the right so that his knee ended up directly beneath his chin. As he did this he allowed the belly button to slide to the right. This action has opened his hips and with them his chest 45 degrees to the flight line.

This is a terrific way to feel the back swing weight shift as we pivot, with the hands on the shoulders we can feel how the body can turn the chest and the hips through the proper use of the feet and knees. When we arrive here as we swing, the hips stop but the shoulders continue to wind until the back is to the target.

Since this drill does not have the hands and arms doing anything the mind can monitor the feels of the weight shift and balance. As you do the drill, focus on the feeling of where the weight is on the feet. Feel the weight flow from centered on the arches over to the center of the right heel and the ball of the left foot. The hips must slide right and the spine must feel to point at the right heel. You should almost, but not quite be able to lift the entire left foot off the ground, some weight should remain on the ball of the left foot.

The only difference between this photo and the photo on the facing page, is that Jim has turned his shoulders. His back is now 90 degrees to the target, ready for the 90 degree return as the legs and feet reverse the weight shift. The look of the left ankle everting can be seen in both of these photos.

As the weight shifts back, the hips will feel to slide in the direction that they are pointing (arrow), and they will turn without feeling as if they turn. As the hips slide the chest must feel to stay wound fully to the right and well behind them. Doing this causes the leg actions and hip rotation, caused by the right foot actions, to turn the chest. The actions described, quickly turn the hips at exactly the correct moment to assist the release.

When the shoulder turn is complete the weight will be mostly on the right heel, what weight remains on the left foot will be on the ball of the foot and the big toe. The heel must not be intentionally lifted, simply freed up to allow the knee to move under the chin as it flexes. At this point the right knee is straight but not quite locked. Fully locking the knee slows our ability to get off the right foot.

This photo shows the exact position we see on the preceding page. Notice that the left shoulder would now be fully turned while the hips would have only turned 45 degrees. The spine pointing at the right heel can be plainly seen. Even though the spine is now leaning toward the target, this is not a reverse weight shift since 95% of the weight is on the right foot. The head is still centered. The mass of the body weight is behind the ball. The wrecking ball action of the lower body slide is in place, and ready to swing forward to re tilt the "T". The levers are lined up and ready to begin the compound leveraged action that powers the triangle.

The Weight Shift In Action

The bottom end of the "T" that represents the spine and shoulders is where the center of mass of the body is located (roughly at the belly button). The mass of the body weight, will be used to power the start of the downswing as the belly button and pelvis slide laterally caused by the hip tilt and leg actions. We will be using this mass of weight in a wrecking ball type action to leverage the left shoulder up by driving the left leg (which is bent in the back swing) vertically, and the left hip laterally. We do this by retracting the knee, not the hip. This drives the left shoulder straight up in a vertical rocking action as the left leg straightens and the right leg shortens. This causes the left arm to rotate first down, and then when the heel turns out, around. The left arm is thus directed 45 degrees across the flight line, and then around and up as the running right leg turns the hips and with them the chest. For this to happen the right heel and knee must immediately lift and bend, the right rib cage can then be pulled close to the top edge of the right hip bone.

The above actions of the right knee, hip and foot the hips must happen or the hips cannot slide and then turn. By sliding the hips laterally instead of turning them we use the mass of the body together with the leverage of the leg actions to move the bottom end of the spine and shoulder "T", creating the correct path of the point of the triangle and also the club.

In the photo above left we see the player with an imaginary spike through his neck, the lateral shift must feel to not bend the spike. There will automatically be a 90 degree turn simply by sliding and reversing the left knee from bent to straight and the right knee from straight to bent. Due to the fact that the hips automatically turn the hips 45 degrees in the direction of the straight leg, the reversal of the knees turns the hips and with them the chest 90 degrees which positions the chest parallel to the flight line for perfectly directed impact. Jim has not moved his arms, notice that the left arm is moved back to the address position simply from the foot and knee action, simply adding the swing of the club with the extending right arm and the forearm twirl the ball sends the ball a long way.

How the Pivot Controls the Perfect Plane

A major problem in all swing types is controlling the downswing plane of the clubhead and the return of the club on the correct inside out swing approach path. This is sometimes a matter of the players perception, due to the players desire to hit the ball directly in the back and drive it straight down the flight line to the target. If you try to swing straight down the flight line you will invariably pull the shot. This is caused by the body having turned farther left than the mind perceives, since the head is still and we are making no effort to turn. Due to this perceptional problem, the left arm must feel to be swung down a straight line 45 degrees right of the flight line for the swinging club to be travelling straight down the flight line through impact.

If the ball is still pulled left the chest has been rotated left (generally caused by poor heel timing or a lack of the right side lower back muscle contraction) this forces the left arm and hand to come down a higher plane than the one they swung back on. Unlike the standard concept of hitting the ball with chest rotation, our concept will be to hit the ball before we rotate. We will consciously attempt to keep our backs turned to the target, our left arm pinned tightly to the chest in the #7 position with no attempt of the hips, chest or shoulders to turn left.

Of course we will be turning left throughout he hit, due to the run of the right leg around the posted left leg and the outward turn of the left heel. The hip turn (which turns the retarded chest) will be largely un-felt, and will start later and be very quick through impact. This quick turn will be a product of the hip slide as we attempt to bump our left hip against an imaginary wall. As this happens the knees reverse their back swing actions assisted by the quick turn out of the right heel.

Correctly done we will feel to simply be replanting the left heel as we simultaneously pick up the right heel. Thus stepping from our right foot to our left foot and driving the left shoulder straight up with the vertical and straightening left leg. The hips must slide laterally left as the left knee posts, the bottom leg of the "T" must move. To assist this as we lift the right heel we pull the right shoulder down and back as if into the right hip pocket, using the lower back muscle. The right side ribs, due to this, will be pulled close to the right hip due to the contraction of the right side lower back muscles. This action slides the hips, slightly arches the back and allows the, now shortened, entire right side of the body to rotate between the spine and the ball and thus put all of our body weight as well as our leg and arm muscular strength into hitting the ball. The plane then is perfectly controlled as is the clubface due to our hand and forearm actions.

The Clubhead Path And The Plane

A wise traveler once told me that if I missed my plane I would not get the flight that I had planned for. The plane controls the path of the clubhead, if we miss it we will have to take a different flight. Hopefully if we miss our plane we will still arrive at the planned for destination on time. This is possible but unlikely.

The plane of the golf club that Ben Hogan envisioned (flat piece of glass sitting on the shoulders and angled down to the ball), is the basis of the concept of controlling the clubhead approach path. This path controls the direction of the clubhead as it passes through the impact area. Since the clubhead must be square to the flight line at impact and travelling straight down it. It is vital to be on the correct plane and also the correct path. The ability to return the clubhead on the correct path can be learned by first understanding that the energy of the pivot must bring the left arm down plane at an angle to the ground and also to the line of flight. The angle of the left arm toward the ground is controlled by the angle of the spine as the weight shifts from foot to foot. The path of the energy will feel to be 45 degrees down toward the earth and out toward the ball at 45 degrees across the line of flight as if we are swinging the left arm toward right field. The rotation of the hips bends the straight path into a curved one. This can be seen in the photo on page 124, The clubhead arc on the downswing goes out, but the turn of the hips bends it and brings it back in.

Since the spine has the lower end sliding laterally, first to the right to get the weight on to the straight up and down post of the right leg, as we swing back during the back swing, the arms will swing upward without lifting them as they follow the shoulder turn. To return the club on the correct plane the weight must shift all of the way forward to get the weight on top of the straight left leg post, before the hips, and with them the shoulders, turn. The result will feel to be a downward and cross line angled direction of the driven left arm and hand. We call this action the left hand delivery path. This delivery path of our energy will cause the clubhead to start down on the right plane and also cause the clubhead to follow the correct path. The late happening turn of the hips, rotates the chest and with it the driven left arm. This bends the straight cross line path, into an arc that travels straight down the flight line during the impact release sequence.

Imagine a clock face drawn on the ground beneath you, with noon where the ball is and your head over the pin. Swinging down you should feel to be sliding the hips from 4 to 10 across the clock (page 109). The un-felt rotation of the retarded chest caused by the hips will direct the releasing clubheads energy directly into the back of the ball.

The Lateral Hip Slide

Starting down with a slow lateral slide of the hips, with no attempt to turn either the hips or the shoulders toward the flight line, is essential to control the correct inside to square clubhead path. If the lateral hip slide as the weight shifts forward to the left post is not completed before the hips and chest begin to turn toward the flight line the left arm will not follow the correct path to the ball and will cause the club to approach the ball from outside the flight line. This is the commonly termed over the top move, it produces a variety of wild shots, from the pull to the slice. If the hands are fully released the pull will happen, if the clubface is held square to the flight line the slice will happen. Between these two extremes are a wide variety of bad shots all traceable to not making a good lateral slide, and the compensating actions the hands will make to save the shot.

The slow lateral slide shifts the body from a one foot balance on the straight right leg to a one foot balance on the straightening left leg, it also creates the needed early massive force to start the entire lever assembly moving. It automatically creates the correct path for the downswing and correctly done drives the left arm all of the way from the top of the back swing to and beyond impact. The turn of the body to the left is delayed when we first slide laterally from one foot to the other. Due to that the delayed spin of the hips to the left happens quickly. The hip turn, due to this delay, then happens when it does the most good; during the moment of impact. Since the hips turn late, the entire turning action of the body is also delayed. This allows both an easier task of staying behind the ball until impact and a powerful rotational force during the time when it is most needed.

Since the turn does not start until the downswing is well under way the body rotation is quicker due to simple time management. If two things travel a distance or rotate an amount in the same amount of time, but one does not begin its movement until after the other, the delayed one must move quicker to finish at the same time. This is best illustrated by the following analogy.

If two runners were to have a race, and one had a head start, yet both arrived at the finish line together it would be easy to see that the runner who ran farther had to go faster. By using the lateral shift before the hip turn we both gain the power of the body weight and also increase the speed of the body rotation at the moment of impact. The later you start the quicker you must go to finish on time.

I know these pages repeat the same thing, said several different ways, but since doing it correctly is so vital to the action I feel that it cannot be overstressed.

The Feel Of The Direction Of The Hip Slide

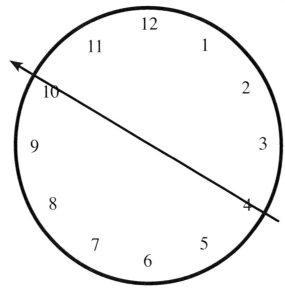

As we step from the straight, but flexing right leg to the straightening left leg the laterally sliding hips must feel to travel on the 4 to 10 line, This keeps the body from turning prematurely and controls the correct plane and path to the club.

The feeling of pulling the right shoulder blade into the right hip pocket bunches the stretched right side spinal erector muscles, and causes the left hip to slide left and the back to get a slight arch.

This action causes the left arm to feel to travel along the same arrow, as we start the down swing. This creates the correct beginning to the arc that the clubhead will follow. The die is cast. If the beginning of the start down is flawed the arc will be flawed since it is impossible to repair that error once made.

The slow lateral slide combined with the lifting of the right heel as the left heel slams down and the shortening of the lower right side back muscles creates the perfect plane and arc. Learning this series of actions is crucial, since any error made in the start down cannot be repaired during the rest of the swing.

Only after this action is mastered can we begin to speed up the lateral slide to increase distance. There is no reason to try to rush this learning process, since correctly done the slow lateral shift still supplies more than ample power.

The extra power of a larger and faster slide of the hips will be easier to make several months down the line when this move is grooved and the timing of the right knee and hand release is perfected. Even then it should be used sparingly.

THE FORMULA FOR POWER AND ACCURACY

A very strong bowler could stand right at the foul line and because of this could be very accurate at getting his ball started on the right board and thus be on line. His ball speed due to his size and strength would perhaps be adequate.

Smaller bowlers however would have less speed and thus not be able to deliver the impact energy to the pins that the bigger player would.

The Bowler

THE FORMULA FOR POWER AND ACCURACY

What's Bowling Got To Do With It?

Several years ago I was teaching a group lesson of complete beginners. When I teach beginner's I always try to relate golf to some sport or activity they have had experience with. Usually baseball or some other common activity that involves throwing or one with some leg movements like running, I would then explain how those motions work in the portion of the swing that they already knew how to do.

One man said "I was a professional bowler" I was stumped, kept a straight face and went on to the next student. I could not think of a single thing that golf had in common with bowling, boy was I wrong.

About a week later one of my students (a pro who plays mini tours) came to see me. His problem was hitting solid shots that went right or left of his target, he had tried lots of different fixes but could not put a finger on what needed fixing.

After 3 or 4 swings I could see that he was out of position at impact, for a few different reasons depending on which of several swings I saw. I knew instantly that the problem was from both the pivot and an unwind of the body,

I said look at this position, as I posed in a position just before the impact position, I had my chest parallel to the flight line and my lower body turned well left of it. My arms were both to the right of my body (left arm back across the chest in the #7 position. You will learn about these positions and actions later and when you re-read the book this paragraph will make perfect sense.

Keeping my chest turned as far right of my hips as I could I then rotated my hips further around until my chest was facing the target, I said see I want you at impact to feel just like you were bowling the ball........I had an epiphany, I knew that I could better explain the swing and the release to my beginners, little did I know what I would learn as I began to think more and more about it.

So, how is golf like bowling? We will start with the similarities of what the hands do as we swing the club or roll the bowling ball.

To better understand the actions, the coming sketches will remind you of the cone and why we use it.

Same Arm Effort / More Ball Speed

 To partly understand why we pivot, lets look to the actions of a bowler. A big strong man could stand right at the foul line and, using only the strength of his arm and upper body, he could throw the ball down the lane. Let's say he rolls the ball at 25 mph. To increase the speed of the ball, he could retreat several yards and run up to the foul line while throwing the ball. If he could attain the speed of 8 mph, the ball would now be rolling at 33 mph. This is a 25% increase. A 25% speed increase creates at least a 25% harder impact.

The same is true for a golfer, if he can run past the ball in a small circle he can add speed to the rotation of the axle (spine). Turning the axle faster brings the arms around like spokes. The hands arrive to impact going faster and thus can swing the clubhead much faster. This is explained graphically with the sketches on the later pages.

Our bowler having retreated to the beginning of the lane, can now run up and gain 7 or 8 mph of body speed to his 25 mph arm speed and thus increase his ball speed by roughly 25%. His ball speed would now be 32 or 33 mph and will be much more powerful.

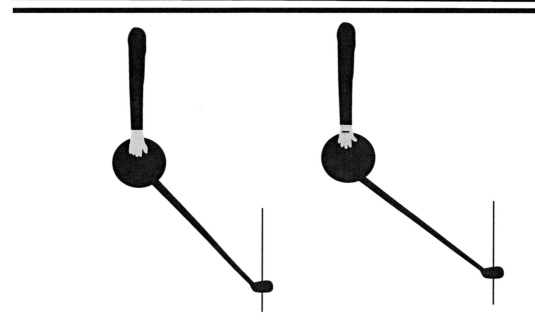

These sketches show a side view of hands holding bowling balls with golf clubs attached, notice that no matter the club, long or short the action is the same.

Below left I show what happens as the right wrist cocks the club and rotates the ball in preparation to give it energy. The sketch (bottom right) shows the hand and clubs motion as it goes forward in an underhand throwing type release.

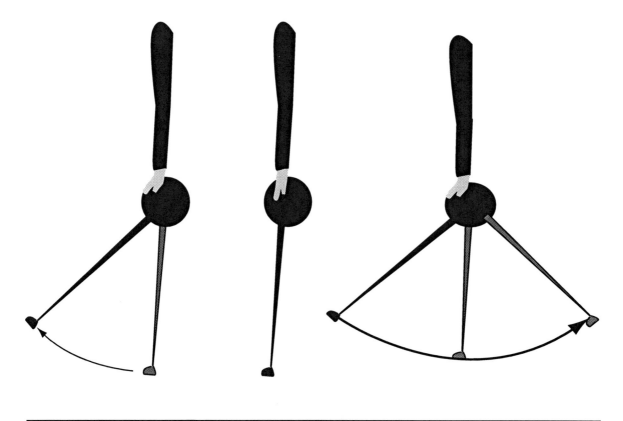

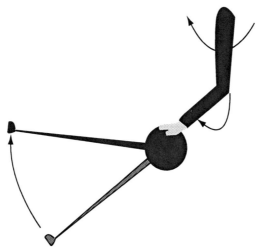

The arm actions in these 2 sketches give a visual of what our right arm does in the swing. In these sketches we see what happens when the upper arm bone rotates inside the shoulder socket as the arm swings back and up. This happens as the right arm folds into the arc caused by the length of the left arm. Below we see what happens to the right arm if it turns and folds properly. The arm actions on this page will be easily understood the second time that you read the book.

If the arm simply swings back and up we arrive here, a position from where we can swing the ball down, around, under and up and hit effective shots with just one hand. Try it, its easy. We must first learn to feel how we can swing the club back in the above manner if we want it to return in the reverse of this motion.

The top of the back swing position will find the club and the right arm not quite looking like this due to the fact that when the right forearm winds up the left arm affects where it can go.

Bowler

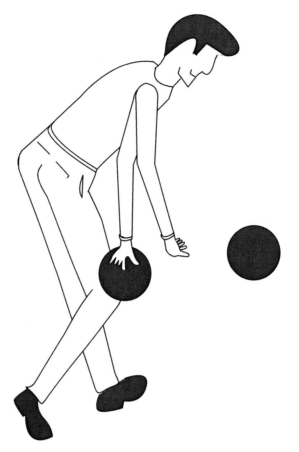

Here we have a bowler releasing his ball down the lane, notice that before the release his palm faces the floor, after release his palm faces skyward. This type release gives the ball roll with no spin. If the right forearm turns the hand so that an observer sees the back of the right hand the ball turns left due to the spin, but if the palm simply turns up, the ball rolls straight.

This is the way we release the club using the conical action. When we get to this position the only difference's between the bowler and the golfer is that the left hand is on the club, rather than just helping to hold balance. The golfers body positions (next page) are very similar, notice that all of the body weight is on the straight left leg. Notice also that the right foot is all of the way up on the toe. If his left foot were turned more to the right as a golfers is, the lifting of the right heel and the rotation of the right foot out and around would have turned the hips to where they are here. As in bowling the release is along side of the right hip,. Also as in bowling the right hand never gets in front of the body until after the release. Notice that the right knee gets there with the ball.

Golfer

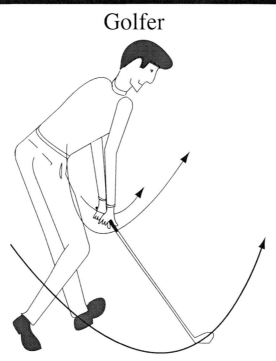

This is the same drawing with a golf club substituted for the bowling ball. If the right hand rolls over the left the ball hooks. Since the right hand is closer to the ball than the left hand it must pass between the left hand and the ball. By allowing the left wrist to release in a flapping manner, the right hand can make the bowler type release and throw the clubhead through the ball. The body position could have been drawn slightly differently to better emulate the golfers balanced position, (The golfer in the sketch would be out of balance) but it illustrates my point. I could have chosen a softball pitcher to illustrate this action, but the bowler and his run up more closely resembles what we are doing.

The hit closely resembles a hockey players slap shot, or a polo riders hit. I toss this in for those who have had these experiences. The way we swing the club is similar to the polo riders swing in that it is alongside of him rather than in front of him. Notice that our bowler (above), if he were riding a horse, would be able to swing the club in the arc shown without hitting the horse. The club would clear the horses right buttock on the down swing, and also miss his head as the club swung through and up. The horse would not let you hit it in the head with your golf club twice. The polo rider uses only the right arm as he swings, in the 21st Century golf swing we will also swing as if with only the right arm. The left arm must accommodate this, it only functions as a guide, just as the tether on the maypole simply restrains the balls straight line travel and changes its motion and direction into a circle. Our energy sends it straight like the bowler, the rotating point of the triangle creates the size, direction and speed of the clubheads orbit.

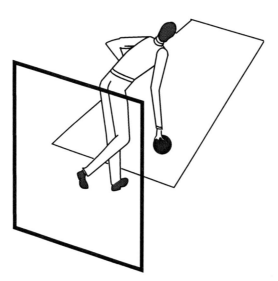

In these 2 sketches we see our bowler standing at the foul line as if ready to throw the ball down the lane, The square represents a glass wall, as if the run up lane were very short and the pane of glass would restrict his back swing.

In the lower sketch we see that our bowler cannot swing his arm straight back since the glass is too close and the resulting swing back would shatter the glass.

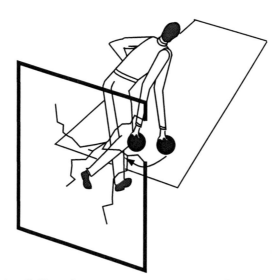

In the 2 sketches on the following page we can see that our bowler could make a curving arc from the shoulder socket and turn the body (notice the hip turn) to swing the ball back and miss the glass.

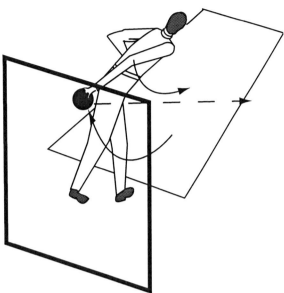

To throw the ball down the lane, he simply steps forward to his left foot. The natural return rotation of the hips would then cause him to throw the ball down the lane, he would again have more power and speed than with the restricted back swing caused by the sheet of glass. The releasing action of the golf swing must coincide with the rotation of the hips, which is a product of the right leg running around the left leg. Done with correct timing the hips keep the chest turning and provide much power. An important similarity between the golfer and the bowler is that the ball never gets out in front of the bowler before he gets all of the way to the foul line, just as the golfer would never get the club back around in front of the body until after impact.

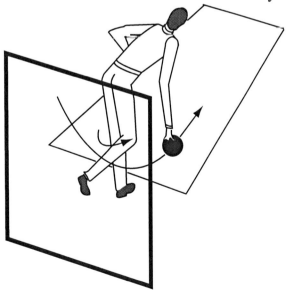

THE FORMULA FOR POWER AND ACCURACY

Combining The Units

THE FORMULA FOR POWER AND ACCURACY

Creating A Golf Swing By Assembling The Parts

We will now begin to join the 3 Units to create a complete golf swing.

Review the 1/8 and 1/4 shots before you attempt to make the 3/8 shot, this shot and the 1/2 shot to follow need to be done correctly to begin to tie the parts into a whole.

Once learned the 1/2 shot contains all of the elements of a full drive minus the fuller shoulder turn and follow through, due to that it is an extremely important shot to practice. Much practice should be spent on this shot, it will groove the body positions and timing so necessary for full swing perfection.

Do not neglect the other partial shots. These partial shots will prove to be excellent in getting the ball up and down should the full swing miss fire. Due to the extreme difficulty of the game as well as the fact that we are human and cannot expect to swing perfectly every time, recovery shots are inevitable.

Connecting Units 1-2 and 3

These things need to happen;

• The body moves the triangle

•The triangle shortening the right side as you swing back, and then straightening as you swing through, and the left side doing the mirror image after impact

When you add the club you get the total package.

•The controlled swing of the club itself.

•The right hand passing between the left hand and the ball through impact.

For the ball to be truly well struck, the clubhead must pass the point of the triangle and get ahead of it as soon as possible after impact. This requires the free release of the left wrist that allows the right hand to deliver the tossing action hit, through impact. The sooner the clubhead begins to return after impact the greater the energy transfer and more perfect the hit, assuming square contact.

The 3/8 Shot

The 3/8 shot uses both of the actions of the previously learned shots, and adds the beginning of the left arms movement to the right, as well as the turning of the hips on the way through. The left hand pushes the right hand to a spot several inches (3 to 5) to the right of the right leg. The weight remains on the left foot as in the previous shots, but as we swing the clubhead down the right knee and ankle must run slowly around the straight left leg (see lower right photo facing page). This action, done by the right knee and the lifting and turning of the right heel returns the left hand to and through the address position while the left arm remains in place across the body and just to the right of the right leg. Through impact the hands must travel with the right knee, not before it or after it. This times the actions of the upper and lower halves of the body, and keeps them synchronized with each other.

This shot begins to utilize part of Unit # 3 since the hip turn is involved. This is a critical shot to learn, and is the hardest to get right. This shot teaches keeping the left arm and chest back as the hips turn the chest through. The arm remains exactly in the position that it attains when swung back. It must remain back across the chest so that contact is made when the hands are alongside, or just slightly in front of, the right hip. It teaches that the body turns left simply from the foot and knee action of the right leg as the pelvis rotates on the post of the left leg. This last sentence will make more sense after you have learned about how the pivot drives the arms. To feel this simply lift the right heel and turn it out as you hit. The resulting shot may surprise you by going dead straight.

This shot like the others will go 3/8 as far as the full shot with the same club. If you practice this shot with all your iron clubs you will soon have an arsenal of shots that can predictably fly and roll your ball to the target. Each with a different flight trajectory and roll out distance. High flight short roll and visa versa.

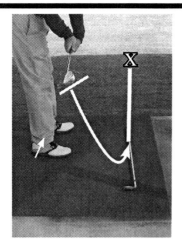  

Timing the Hit

In the 3/8 shot start with most of your weight, solidly on the left leg allow no weight transfer to the right leg. Swing back through the 1/4 shot back swing position to a point where the shoulders have made a small turn and the hands are 6 inches right of the right pants pocket, while the hips have not. Wind the forearms. To start the swing down, shoot the right knee out to right field and turn the right heel out toward the flight line as the hands and arms twirl the club. To maintain the #7 position, the left arm must not swing forward from the shoulder as this happens, the legs must rotate it back down.

Even though the weight never shifted to the right leg as the swing starts down we can see that the right knee and heel have moved. They do not move in the 1/4 shot, but they must move in the 3/8 shot since the hips now must turn to power the hands through. If the right heel and knee do not move the arms swing independently, and we give up the legs abilities to provide direction control and power. In this golf swing the arms travel with the body, not faster than the body.

The hips must turn exactly as the hands hit through. This is the beginning of feeling the timing between the upper and lower halves of the body. The hands must go through with the right knee, not before or after. For the hips to be able to turn correctly, the right heel must free up by lifting and turning out toward the flight line. The clubhead feels to go up and out to point X due to the conical release. Even though it feels to go up and out it remains perfectly on the oblique plane as the turning body rotates the triangle left. Wind up the forearms and twirl the club through, make sure that you fully release the clubhead and hit the ball firmly with your hands. Study all of the arrows in the photos above. As the swing gets larger, the turn simply gets larger and from after impact on in the follow through, the right arm becomes the radius of the arc of the hands.

The 1/2 Shot

The only difference between the 3/8 shot and the 1/2 shot is the weight shift and the additional turn and power it gives. On any shot less than the 1/2 shot the weight does not have to shift, nor should it. If the weight were shifted to the right foot on shots less than the 1/2 shot the player will not have enough time in the downswing to consistently get back on the left foot, and a fat shot is then all too easy to do. If the weight is entirely (except for the weight on the right toe) on the straight left leg at impact fat shots are mostly eliminated.

The 1/2 shot is the full swing in microcosm, all of the parts of the full swing exist in this shot and this shot is the key to both understanding the full motion and is a wonderful way to practice it. By practicing 1/2 wedge shots we are working on one of the most critical shots in the game as it is actually played, we are in effect both working on our driver motion as we improve our ability to get the ball up and down from 50 yards or so. To hit the 1/2 shot all you need to do is allow the weight (belly button) to slide right, extend the right knee to straight as you flex the left knee by pulling it sideways with the muscles on the inside of the upper left thigh. This shifts the weight and tilts the shoulders going back.

Both above photos were taken, without Jim moving a muscle. The weight has shifted to the right foot, the shoulders are turned 45 degrees further than the hips, the club is now parallel to the shoulders and pointing 45 degrees across the flight line. From here all Jim needs to do to hit the ball perfectly is to slam down the left heel, slide the hips laterally while not attempting to turn them and at the exact same moment both pick up the right heel and hit with the right hand. The chest must stay wound to the right of the hips until after the ball is struck to get the legs and hips involved in the action. All of this although described piecemeal will soon be easy to do as a one piece operation. These shots are the very best way to build the swing and at the same time build a solid short game so if you do not hit a perfect shot you can still make your par anyway.

By simply replanting the left heel, pulling the left knee back under the left hip, and simultaneously raising the right knee and heel, the hips slide laterally left and begin to turn. As the right heel reaches this point it begins to turn out toward the flight line and continues to rise up on the toe. These actions will cause the right leg to run in a small circle thus rotating the hips on top of the posted left leg. The weight shift actions of the feet and knees brings the triangle of the arms and shoulders to here, this was done simply by the foot and knee actions and hip slide. At least 90 percent of the body weight is on the posted left leg at this point. The right arm has already twirled the club 1/4 of the twirl. Notice the clubhead is already facing the ball. The left arm still remains in the same position it was in at the top of the back swing, and the chest is still 45 degrees behind the hips.

Connection has been maintained. The hips are driving the chest, the right triceps is straightening the right arm, and the right wrist is beginning the toss of the release. From here the left wrist must flap to allow the right hand to throw the clubhead through, and the heel must rotate out to turn the hips.

If the left wrist does not release, or the right heel does not rotate out toward the flight line, the shot will be blocked right. The ball will not curve unless the wrists were frozen, it will go straight however it will lose distance, since the body stopped and the club did not pass the hands. The right heel must rotate up on to the toe and out toward the flight line. The right leg will then quickly rotate the hips on the posted left leg, The power of the legs is now driving the hips and with them the chest and left arm. The triangle is beginning to re-form and the clubhead is under heavy acceleration as it races to catch up to the left arm and pass the point of the triangle shortly after impact.

When the ball is struck, the right arm is still straightening, and the left wrist is still slightly bowed, although it is in the act of releasing. The right elbow by straightening rises up to the height of the left elbow through impact thus re-forming the triangle..

In the photo below left the impact position begins, notice the still not quite straight right elbow and still slightly bowed left wrist. Below right just after impact the right arm is straight and the left elbow is flexing downward. The left wrist has flapped showing the complete release. Notice that the right hand and right knee went through exactly together.

The right arm at this point takes over the job of maintaining the radius of the arc of the hands. The left wrist completely flaps to allow the pendulum to swing as the left elbow relaxes and folds, done this way the left arm simply gets out of the way. The clubhead as it releases passes the point of the arm shoulder triangle without closing. The forearms nearly touch at the wrists as this happens. The triangle re-forms for only the briefest of instants as the club swings through. Immediately after re-forming the left side of the triangle collapses.

In the above right photo, due to the fullness of the wrist flap release, the wrists are nearly touching each other. The clubhead has already passed the point of the triangle and it actually is beginning to come back in, to go up over the left shoulder, while the hands are still going toward the target. With this full release of the clubhead without roll, the ball flies dead straight without curvature.

Here we see the result of the raising and the turn out of the heel. The right hip has rotated at exactly the same time that the right hand has hit through. The left arm at this point has begun to flex at the elbow (the left wrist has already released). From here on out the speed left over in the clubhead pulls the player through to the finish.

Notice that the clubhead has not revolved around the shaft, the release is complete and the clubface could only have been square at impact. The entire power of the right arm has been used as it twirled the club, and hit through the impact area. With the car crank wrist release there is no chance of a hook.

Using The Right Arm And Hand

Since the right hand is farther down the shaft, it is closer to the ball than the left hand, due to this it can be used very effectively by having it pass between the left hand and the ball as it hits through. This hand action powerfully drives the last lever in the chain (the golf club) through impact. As seen earlier the right hand must not roll over the left through impact since this would cause a hook. Due to this action, which must occur during the common swing, the right hand and arm has gotten a bad reputation over the years as being a culprit, causing hooks, etc. when mistimed.

Many instructors teach not to use the hit of the right hand and arm, claiming that it cannot be tamed. By not hitting with the right hand power is lost. Others teach that the right hands power should not be used until the hands are "in the hitting area". Doing this loses less power, but is still a loss and the timing of the hit becomes even more difficult to groove.

It becomes visually obvious in the photos of this release that the right hand can be tamed and the full use of its considerable power applied to the ball. For it to work the left wrist must relax and allow the right hand to hit through. If the left hand does not allow the free release while training the hands, a good thought to make this happen is turn the knuckles of the left hand under and up toward the target by using a little muscular effort of the outside of the left forearm (pg 53). This action would cause the left palm to turn down and face the ground just after impact. For the pendulum to swing, the left wrist must not be locked, it must be a well oiled axle.

In our swing we use the power of the right arm and hand completely, by starting to use them immediately as the downswing begins. This gives us a head start at applying power and a square clubhead at impact. The effect will be as great as the difference between a standing broad-jump and a running broad-jump. Much more distance will be covered.

The release has three functions. First, it begins the clubhead catching up to the left arm which is already on its way to the ball driven by the pivot. Second, it frees up the right arm to straighten. Third, as the hands reach the ball the flapping motions of the releasing wrists, send the clubheads energy into the ball. Done this way the release occurs more naturally and fluidly through impact, simply by giving the clubhead a light twirl to start it. The natural unwinding of the right forearm and the straightening of the right arm produces square contact with much zip. Since the clubhead remains square to the hit, the ball flies straight and true with only pure backspin.

THE FORMULA FOR POWER AND ACCURACY

The Use Of The Right Arm Levers

As we return the left arm down the perfect inside out plane by the proper pivot, we start the downswing with the twirl. This twirling action caused by unwinding the forearms begins the clubheads rotation around the point of the arm shoulder triangle, but does not include the flapping release action of the wrist axles just yet. Part of what this action does is rotate the elbow of the right arm into a position near the right hip. From there the combined actions of the right triceps extension and the bowling ball release action of the wrist as the forearms fully unwind gives us a motion similar to throwing a screw ball as done by a softball pitcher. You can add power with a drive of the right triceps and a toss.

The above 3 photos show the forearm unwind and underhand screwball action of the right forearm through impact. The lower bone of the right forearm (Ulna) rotates from behind the upper bone (radius) to ahead of it as the right hand throws. The left lower arm bone rotates also in a counter clockwise direction as the hands release, this important action helps the left upper arm to rotate from within the shoulder socket, thus allowing the left arm to collapse and clear.

These combined actions allow us to create a perfect arc of the clubhead with a wide sweeping down under and up releasing motion through the hitting area. Once learned the ball will fly straight, high and far with little or no side spin and with the ideal desired amount of backspin. We will have a motion that will repeat and the more that you trust it the better it gets, conversely the better it gets the more you will trust it. It will feed off itself like some strange alien life form. Gone will be the fear of a slice or a hook, Golf will seem a pleasure rather than work. You will have the distance and accuracy to play an attacking game rather than a defensive one.

Modern thinking creates a swing that is easier on the body, more reliable under pressure, more powerful and takes less effort. You will get more power out of this swing with less effort than with any other method.

The Shoulder Blades

As the swing gets larger, the tromboning actions of the arms and the winding of the forearms causes the shoulder blades to slide on the body. We call these actions abducting (going away from the spine) and adducting (getting close to the spine). These movements allow the point of the triangle to get fifteen to twenty degrees farther to the right of the center of the body. By doing this they increase the depth of the turn by a significant amount. You will know that you have moved the shoulders correctly when the left shoulder blade is as far as it can get from the spine and the right shoulder blade is as close as it can get to the spine. Have a friend look at you from behind when you are at the top of a full back swing, your right scapula should be much closer to the spine than the left. When in this position the left arm will be tight to the chest, and the shoulder will have moved about 15 degrees in front of a straight line drawn across the rib cage.

The right upper arm must rotate within the shoulder socket and attain a position that is as close as your physique will allow it to being straight with your chest. To see this right arm position see the lower photo on page 144. If you are broad in the chest or have either short arms or extra wide shoulders your right arm may look more like the photo on the top on that same page. Every player has his or her own best top of the back swing position based on their own physical limitations. The position shown on the photo below is the ideal, and even if you can only reach the position shown in the photo on the top, you should mentally be trying to emulate that right arm position.

As you wind the forearm focus on the feeling of retracting the right arm to the top right photo position. Direct your attention to the feel of the right scapula trying to touch the spine. Try to get the right hand as far back and to the right as you can. Doing these things will stretch the muscles that locate the scapula and will allow the left arm to set in your tightest #7 left shoulder position. Returning to the ball the left scapula must remain in this away from the spine position, to strike the ball with the club far to the right of our center.

On the following page we see G.J. about half way down, the #7 is intact. If he simply turned left on his left leg the club which is now directly along side of him would impact the ball, as if a long nail went down through the shoulder through the hip and left foot. The rotating hips would then be driving the chest and tightly pinned left arm, slamming the ball with a long lever that has the lower part of the lever below the hinge rapidly catching up as the right arm straightens. This lower lever has a rapidly twirling clubhead attached to the end of it as it rotates under, with the clubface square, in the conical release.

THE FORMULA FOR POWER AND ACCURACY

The Forearms And The Thumbs

As we swing the club back to the top of the back swing, we will control the club with the actions of the forearms and the thumbs. By focusing on the forearms and thumbs we will fully control the face of the club and the actual actions of the arms and shoulders during the back swing. Correctly done the club will go up and into the perfect slot every time, these motions will also help control the positioning of the arms. The natural unwinding of the wound up muscles as we swing down will direct and control the always square clubface through the hit.

Starting back these are the things we will focus on and the order that you read them will be the order that you do them.

1. Tuck the left pinky under as you set the right wrist straight back, without raising the thumbs. The thumbs should move 45 degrees right.

2. While holding the left wrist firm in the slightly bowed condition caused by move #1 wind the right forearm in a counter-clockwise manner while making sure to keep the right thumb from raising. As you do these actions allow the arms the freedom to swing freely from the shoulder sockets, and feel the upper right arm bone rotate up and out to the throwing position on page 144.

3. The right thumb sets straight back, and must not raise above the fight forearm bone as the wind-up of the forearm actions occur.

When these moves are learned they will be very easy to repeat and will make it simple to twirl the clubhead in a powerful and controlled arc around the point of the arm and shoulder triangle. These back swing actions must be felt to combine with a pushing motion from the left shoulder and hip, as the left knee breaks in toward the ball. The left shoulder, hip and the extended left arm should feel to be rotating the chest and the arm shoulder triangle as the left palm seeks the turning right shoulder. The feeling of winding up the right forearm must be accompanied with a relaxed upper right arm which flexes and folds into the arc of the left hand. The left arm creates the size of the arc and the path of the hands as the arm shoulder triangle swings the arms back up and around. The right arm creates the opposite (follow through) arc in precisely the same manner after impact. The 2 halves of this motion will create the conical action of the clubhead, with the left arm controlling the right half in the back swing and the right arm controlling the left half after impact.

The # 7 Position

When the shoulder blades have abducted and adducted, and the hands together with the counter rotating forearms have set the club into the proper top of the back swing position, the left arm will be in what we call the # 7 position since the left arm and shoulder resemble the # 7. The shoulders being the top bar of the 7 and the left arm being the leg. Actually the angle between the top bar and the leg of the 7 is quite a bit more acute, but it is a good way of remembering it. The left arm should be pressed tightly against the upper left pectoral muscle.

Once this angle has been attained, the left arm <u>does not move</u> back down from the shoulder socket, it remains pressed against the pec until well after the ball is struck. This makes the left arm rotate like a spoke in a wheel that uses the spine for an axle. The rotating chest axle (spine) is thus driven by the legs. The rotating hips rotate the spine which drives the retarded chest and shoulders like a drive shaft. The legs do this much more powerfully and accurately than the smaller back and trunk muscles do, if the wind up is lost and the shoulders catch the hips. However by releasing these back and trunk muscles later in the action, in a relaxed way, we will not be wasting their power or their motion.

Here we see G.J. Half way down, it is easy to see that the # 7 position of the left arm and shoulder line is still intact. This is a very important part of our concept, <u>the right forearm has been very active ever since the top of the back swing</u>, but the left arm has not lost the # 7. The feet, legs and hips have returned the left arm to here. Notice the hips remain well ahead of the shoulders, showing that the natural turn of the hips has squared the chest so that the arms can swing the clubhead straight down the flight line. From this point the right hand and arm continue to twirl, as the right heel, and knee, turn through with the club swinging freely from the well lubricated wrist axles. The next pages show the actions of the left arm throughout the swing.

Controlling The Cone From The Shoulders

Due to their design the shoulders are well suited to swing in an arc, and control the turning of the arm shoulder triangle. This triangle has two sides (the shoulder line is the base) which alternately fold to allow the triangle to both swing the clubhead away farther and also to put the right arm into a position so that when it re-straightens it can add a powerful hit. Naturally after the hit the left arm must fold to allow the clubhead to complete the swing.

Each half of the rotational center of the conical action is controlled by whichever arm is straight. The photo series explains this, most of it can easily be felt as it happens. **Going back the left arm should feel as if the upper bone is not rotating,** although it does rotate a small amount clockwise. The left forearm, caused by the pinky tuck rotates an equal amount counter-clockwise as the wrists set, **this is felt** as the pinky tuck. The right forearm then winds up, this action gets the left arm to swing under and up as the club rotates up to the top of the back swing. At the top of the back swing the natural wind up of the right arm causes the clubhead to cock a little bit vertically and slightly open. The player need not focus on this part of the action since it can hardly be felt, but it does occur. This slight un-felt vertical cock, and clubface opening, reverses itself without the need for us to control it swinging down, other than to start the twirl.

The power arm (the right for right handed players) rotates the club around the tip of the triangle, and winds up the forearm muscles, in preparation for the twirling action during the downswing, as it does this it ends up in the perfect position for throwing. The right hand ends up directly over the right elbow.

The downswing action of the right arm is a combination of a clockwise twirl, an extension of the right arm and a down under and up right toss type wrist release, in that exact order. The right hand release and the final extension of the straightening right arm will feel as if the action is a throw. After impact the right forearm will continue to rotate in a clockwise direction. The right arm will swing exactly opposite to the path followed by the left arm as it swung back across the chest, thus maintaining the radius of the hands and controlling the forward arc of the cone.

The two halves of this reversing arm action blend together to create the full conical arc. The extended arm and the flexing arm each control one half of the

Toe Of The Club Touches The Wall

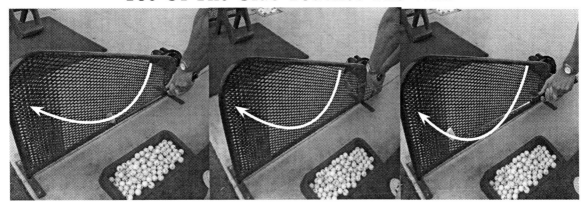

Starting back, the feeling we want is of the toe of the club touching and sliding up a wall as only the wrists flap, as seen above. This by the way is an excellent way of getting a feel for the actions of the hands as the cranking action under the wrist axles allow the club to swing in the bottom section of the cone. The cone can easily be seen and felt by doing this. The photos below shows how the entire left arm and club then swing in a conical action back, under and up in the back swing. This is the feel we want of the clubhead swinging in a large cone. After impact the right arm does the same as it swings forward in a cone from its shoulder socket.

The entire arm once the pinky tucks under must still feel as if we were swinging the club with the toe of the club touching a vertical wall directly in front of the player. Since this occurs with the natural turn it creates the perfect oblique plane for the clubhead. Notice how the left shoulder rotates down and under the chin and the tilt to the right of the lower end of the spine, showing that the weight has shifted. Remember the hand and arm action allows for little vertical wrist cock, only sideways wrist cock and a fully conical action of the entire left arm and club assembly. The arm and club rotate like a spoke which is now bent sideways at the wrist, from the shoulder socket. The winding right forearm and folding right arm relocate it naturally into the perfect top of the back swing position. It will return to the ball perfectly as the actions reverse coming down.

Above left John begins the back swing with the pinky tuck shaft twist motion. On the right he is pushing the club away with the entire left side of his body as he turns behind the ball on the posted right leg. From this point on the final counter-clockwise windup of the forearms, will cause a slight up cock of the left thumb when the right hand is on the club. But it will be limited by the slight left wrist bow.

This drill strengthens the muscles needed to control the shaft of the club as it also trains the proper weight shift and turn. The subtle tilt of the spine target ward of the lower end of the shoulder / spine "T" can be seen. This is the action that tilts the shoulders so that the arms swing up simply by turning the shoulders, they do not have to lift to go up since the axle that they turn on is properly tilted.

Notice that John has not changed the arm shaft angle by lifting the thumb, the arc is broad and correctly controlled. Continue pushing with the left palm seeking the right shoulder, this removes all of the slack between the clubhead and the left heel. Simply by completing the turn of the shoulders, and (if the right hand were on the club) the wind-up of the forearms as the right arm folds creates the perfect top of the back swing position.

What The Left Arm Does In The Full Back swing

Photo #1   Photo #2

The left hand and arm action is a simple tuck of the left pinky knuckle and a rotation under of the entire left arm. The clubhead only moves 45 degrees right of the left hand (photo # 2), and for the rest of the back swing remains in this position relative to the arm. The left arm travels in a sliding across the body and upward rotation directly toward the right shoulder (facing page). It will continue to move in this fashion, until it attains the #7 position at the top. Remember its position is controlled by both a pushing from the left arm and the folding of the right arm as the right forearm winds as the armpit opens.

When both hands are on the club, the thumbs must feel to remain down. Since we never cock the club vertically, lifting the thumbs would lift the clubhead off the plane, The club, then feels to go straight back, with the leading edge of the club slowly rotating under as the club cocks to the right of the point of the arm shoulder triangle. The club and left arm then swing like a sideways bent spoke in a large cone from the left shoulder. This description would describe exactly what the right arm does beyond impact if the descriptive words like right and left were reversed. As the clubhead swings through, the clubface comes from slightly de-lofted to square and with the proper loft. After impact the loft increases as the club lays back due to the right hand reversing the actions of the left hand, moving from photo 2 toward photo 1 (above). In other words the swing is symmetrical, what happens on one side of the ball happens in reverse on the other.

The right thumb keeps the club down and away from the player, by not cocking vertically. The left wrist must remain in the slightly bowed condition to both keep excess vertical wrist cock out and also to enable the wrist hinge release.

THE FORMULA FOR POWER AND ACCURACY

At the top of the back swing you must feel as if the club is in the right hand and in the throwing position, the left arm does nothing coming down. From the position at the top the right hand and arm reverse their actions all of the way to the ball and then mirror image the back swing actions to the finish, with the exception of not moving the right humerus bone forward until after impact. The twirling feel of the right hand and arm, in the downswing, will be as if opening a door knob as the arm extends. Through the hit it will feel as if we are ripping the knob out of the door and continuing to turn the knob as the right hand throws through. The natural returning action, as the stretched muscles work and the bunched muscles relax will move the extending right arm, unwinding forearms and free swinging wrists through the ideal positions as they reverse the back swing actions. Their pre-programmed, and naturally occurring actions control the motion and add much speed as they release the clubheads power through the impact area, and also through the ball.

The above statement is only true if the lever assembly swings freely through impact, and after impact duplicates the tromboning movements in reverse as the left arm trombones and the club returns over the left shoulder. The left hand will pass through the cop saying stop position seen in the photo on page 147.

Doing this correctly will allow all of the energy we have given the clubhead to flow into the ball. Conversely if we impede the swinging clubhead in any way we will slow it down and thus lose distance and also affect accuracy.

When we combine this series of movements with the full use of Unit #3 you will have an action that returns the triangle with collapsing and extending sides as the club twirls around the triangles point.

In this photo series we see the final release of the wrists as they un-hinge sideways. Many things are happening here. The hands are freely releasing, the hips and thus the chest are turning and the right arm is straightening. Notice also that the hands are traveling through the impact area exactly at the same time that the right knee is traveling through the same area. This shows that the arms are traveling at the same speed as the body, not faster than it. The pivot returns the triangle exactly like an axle rotates the spokes. If the spokes travel faster than the axle the timing breaks down, and the power source (the legs) becomes disconnected from the twirling action of the hands. The timing of the hit becomes much easier when the upper half of the action works in time with the lower half.

Here we can see that the clubhead has passed the point of the triangle, notice that the left forearm has not rotated (the wrist watch still faces the target). The right hand has thrown the clubhead through, for this to happen the left wrist must be relaxed and free to flap (the left palm faces the ground after impact). The left elbow must also be free and relaxed, so that it too can bend and get out of the way so as to not slow down the speeding clubhead. From this point on in the swing the clubheads residual speed pulls the player around and up to the finish position. Notice that although the hands are still going toward the target the clubhead is already coming back. This is a full free release.

The photos above show the club angled more, when the right forearm wind up is added this is where it ends up. The hand is under the club and the right arm humerus bone simply returns with the body. The right forearm begins to unwind immediately with the shift of weight. As the axle of the body (spine) turns, the arm rotate like the spokes in a wheel. The right arm, although actively throwing the clubhead, never forces the left arm off the chest until after impact.

As the body approaches impact the right wrist tosses and reverses the slight bow of the left wrist that the tuck of the left pinky created. The club rapidly passes the point of the arm shoulder triangle with the face perfectly square, and traveling rapidly. The right wrist extends as if tossing, just after impact the left arm leaves the chest and the left elbow flexes allowing the right arm to control the finish arc.

The work of the legs was done before impact. Now the chest, arms, shoulders, and the forearms unwind as the clubhead continues the release. The resulting swing is efficient, good looking, powerful and easy on the body.

The Look Of The Top Of The Back Swing

The position we attain at the top of the back swing will determine how our actions back to the ball will have to proceed to hit a good shot. What I mean by this is that good shots can be hit in a variety of ways. However some of these ways require a different way of doing things. To get the full value of this swing it must use all of the parts of this action and no others.

If you do not set the club properly, for this method, you will not be in a good position to return the club solidly into the back of the ball. As a matter of fact, from some positions at the top getting back to the ball properly is nearly impossible. To get an understanding and a feel for why we want the slight bow to the left wrist it pays to look to the top of the back swing position.

To utilize the free release of the wrists without the roll of the forearms the left wrist, at the top cannot be in a cupped position, it must be slightly bowed. This is simple to understand if you think of what we do as we release. Since we release the bow of the left wrist through impact, it is vital to not be in the after the release (left wrist flapped forward) position at the top. That hand and wrist position is where we will be after impact at the end of the arm swing, the finish. The standard swing allows a cupped left wrist position at the top, it must be accompanied by a forearm roll coming back to square the clubface, this brings the timing of the roll into play. It also puts the right arm and hand into a position that restricts their ability to add power.

This has been considered good, since instructors, over the years, in trying to keep the over the top downswing move out of the swing have come up with this position to weaken the right hands use. The right hand has been given a bad reputation, with terms like too much right hand being used to account for a hook or pull. We heartily agree with the great Ben Hogan who said "I wish I had three right hands". Personally I want four or five.

The right hand power is plentiful, and in this swing we use it to the max. The act of making the clubhead catch up to the left arm is not left to gravity and centrifugal force alone as is the case in the late type release. By twirling the clubhead and firing the right arm and hand, in that order, starting as the pivot commences we gain a big head start in applying power. The right arm and hand cannot be used too early or too hard if the pivot is properly executed.

The photo series starting on the following pages graphically illustrates the right hand positions of each type action.

THE FORMULA FOR POWER AND ACCURACY

The Hand Position At The Top

First swing back to the top with the common back swing (cupped left wrist) and vertical wrist cock, once there remove the left hand. Just from the feel of the club in your right hand you will know that you can not use your right hand with any authority from this position. Now swing back to the top using our takeaway, (get the slightly bowed left wrist and fully wound right forearm), again remove the left hand. From this position you can instantly feel what you will be able to do with the right hand, you can use it starting at the top to accelerate the club all of the way through the hit and beyond.

I suggest that you learn how to hit the golf ball from the top of the back swing with only one hand. Start learning how to do this by using only the right hand to hit with. After several attempts you will soon find that it will be nearly impossible to do from the weaker standard position. This is because the standard swing position is designed to keep the right hand and arm out of the swing.

We want use the power and the precision that the right hand and arm can give. It is for these reasons that we do not want the right arm in the standard position. At first you will find that it is also difficult to do from the our position, if the right arm is moved toward the ball from the shoulder socket. Keep the upper right arm bone (the Humerus) from swinging forward. As the right arm swings down it straightens, as these things happen the body turns and the forearm unwinds in a throwing motion. Hit the ball off the right hip (photo page 140) and you soon will be able to hit shots 60 to 80 percent as far as if you used 2 hands.

A similar drill can be learned using only the left arm, although training the left arm is not as necessary as the right since it only responds to the throw in a leash like fashion. It is however important to train the left wrist to be vertical as the release occurs and the right hand passes through, to guarantee squareness of clubface contact. Remember the left wrist has a slight bow until impact, where it releases its energy. To feel the correct action feel the left knuckles turn forward and up through the hit. (Photos page 53). The left palm should face the ground just after the hit. This can more easily be done in the shorter pitch type shots and I recommend that you learn it there. Ultimately you should learn to hit the ball with either hand. The power using the left arm alone will not be as great as the right hand alone due to the relative weakness of the left forearm muscles versus the entire right arm. Some time spent learning to hold the #7 position helps. See the photo sequence for the one handed shot on pages 140.

This is the position you get at the top when you use the vertical wrist cock and forearm roll actions. It requires a reversing of those motions to return the club to square for correct club / ball contact. The release of the wrists and roll of the forearms must be perfectly timed to hit a perfect shot. Errors are easy to make, and practice is required to keep the swing in tune.

From this position at the top, the right hand is not in a good position to add power. Prove it to yourself, go to this position with both hands on the grip, make sure you have the left wrist cupped. Now take the left hand off without changing the right hands position, try to hit the ball with just the right hand. You will see for yourself just how hard this is.

This is the position you get at the top when you use the counter rotation back swing. Notice that the left wrist has a very small bow, this is the perfect top of the back swing. From this position the right hand can power the club, and the left hand can guide it. The left wrist can release by flapping. Completely unlike the left wrist, at the top of the back swing on the preceding page; from that cupped and thumb raised position the wrist cannot release because it is already released. The left wrist releases from a slight bow to a fully cupped position. Since the right wrist releases by throwing the clubhead past the hinging left wrist axle, it goes from a fully cocked back position to a slight bow just after impact. These actions are what allows us to throw the clubhead through the impact area. With a cupped wrist at the top this cannot happen. You cannot close a door that is already closed.

When the left hand is removed from this top of back swing position the right hand is in a very powerful position to twirl and the throw the club. Try hitting balls with only your right hand from this position and you will see how much easier it is to control and swing the club from this position. Hitting one handed shots is hard at first and will take a little practice, but is much easier from this position.

Here Is A Photo Study Of What The Hands Do, Without the Club to Cloud the View

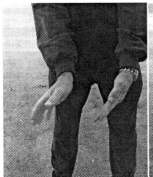  

When seen without the club the concept of how the club swings can easily be grasped. Notice that the forearms rotate in the opposite direction to the commonly conceived swing. This action uses more muscles, and increases the arc of the clubhead by causing the right elbow to rotate out to a throwing position.

  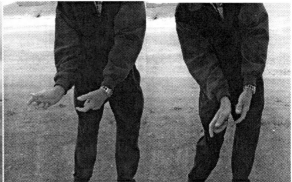

As the body turns and the hands counter-rotate the right forearm swings up on top of the elbow (First 2 photos this row from left). This swings the left arm up to shoulder high or just a little higher depending on body type. The left elbow rotates out in the mirror view of this in the follow through (2 bottom right pics).

In the photo series shown here, the way that the hands feel to relate to each other can easily be seen. When the forearms unwind correctly the left elbow swings up and out of the way. Note that the right hand always stays farther from the swing circle center than the left hand throughout the entire swing.

THE FORMULA FOR POWER AND ACCURACY

How To Throw With The Right Arm

The photo above left shows the right arm in the perfect position from which to make a twirling throw, here is how you use it. Simply leave the upper arm bone (humerus) right where it is and pivot the body, the club will arrive to the ball alongside the right hip, since that is where the right arm now is and if not moved will be. As the right arm comes around with the entire upper body it has much force, versus swinging it with the muscles of the chest and shoulder. If the player uses this body return of the entire right arm gravity and centrifugal force will naturally straighten it. The only other arm movement necessary to swing the club is to smoothly unwind the right forearm in the direction of the arrow. Swinging down using only the right arm lets you feel how the right arm will work in the proper swing.

In the photo on the right the player has brought the club around by moving the upper bone of the arm, this is a big mistake. Once the right upper arm moves forward using it correctly is impossible.

Try this one arm swing yourself, it will take a little practice, but it will teach you not to move the right arm forward. The reason for that is simple, any forward movement of the right upper bone will cause a similar movement to the #7 position. If that happens the point of the triangle will be travelling faster (rpm wise) than the spine. The spoke will be traveling faster than the hub. This disconnects the hands from the driving force of the pivot. To swing well requires a twirl of the club around the point of the triangle as that point is driven around by the body. If the arms move and destroy the #7 position the triangle begins re forming to early destroying any chance of using the chain reaction so necessary for solid golf shots. By leaving the arms back and using the hands to twirl the clubhead we get the best of both worlds, body force and clubhead speed.

The Cop Saying Stop Position

The photos above and below show an arm and hand position we call the "cop saying stop position". This position is one that we must attain to allow the wrists to properly set and the right arm to trombone correctly going back (left photo). The position is equally important going through to allow the wrists to properly release and the left elbow to properly trombone. Simply learning to pose in these positions will help create the correct arm actions as we swing back and through. Notice the full release of the wrist axles (below right).

How it looks with both hands on the club

In the photos on the top you can see the cop saying stop position, in the photos on the bottom the player feels the cop saying stop position. Since the hands are on the club one below the other it looks slightly different, but feels the same.

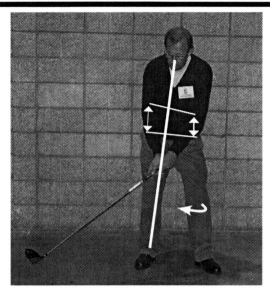

To make the full swing simply make the 1/2 swing larger on both sides. A bigger back swing, with a fuller shoulder turn and a more complete finish is all that you need. The timing of the swing simply requires the twirl to start right from the top and the strike to occur as the right knee passes the ball. The photos with their captions will show these actions and explain them much more clearly than text alone.

As the back swing begins, pull back the right knee to straighten the right leg. As this happens the left knee flexes to point behind the ball, and the lower back muscle on the left side pulls the left lowest rib down toward the top of the left hip bone. (See arrows). Due to these actions the left side of the torso shortens and the right side lengthens. These actions tilt the hips. The right side of the body will lengthen as the ribs move away from the right hip bone. This tilting of the hips causes the hips to slide to the right and points the spine directly at the right heel.

It causes the lower end of the "T" formed by the shoulder and spine to tilt as if a nail were driven through the intersection. This lowers the left shoulder, raises the right shoulder and sets the correct spine angle so that the when the shoulders turn they do so on the proper plane. This action creates the perfect single plane back swing. When the hips tilt the spine correctly and the spine angle is set, the perfect path for the arms in the back swing is controlled by turning the shoulders on the angle that they are now on. The shoulders, arms and hands do not lift the club, they wind up. They do not pull the club in or lift the club up. They simply wind up as they follow the turn of the shoulders. These simple actions complete the perfect single plane back swing. The left shoulder will end up directly below the chin, and the arms will not have to be raised to swing up, they will swing up, simply due to turning on the correct tilt.

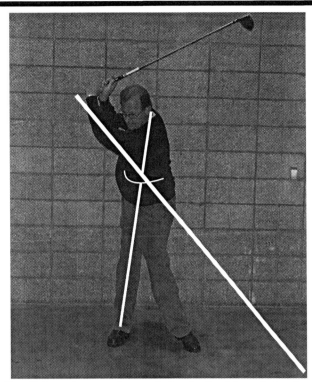

Here we see the result of the shortening of the left side of the body, the left side ribs are very close to the hip bone. At the top of the back swing the head remains between the feet, the hips have turned 45 degrees, the back will have turned 90 degrees to the target line. Since Dan is 66 years old, and is not quite as limber as he once was, the head has turned a little to the right. The wind-up is complete and swinging down the wound up relationship between the hips and the chest must be maintained.

The Unit # 3 actions in the downswing are initiated by the slow lateral slide of the hips, caused by a replacing down of the left heel and at the same exact instant a lifting of the right heel. As this happens the hips must re-tilt caused by the shortening of the right side internal trunk muscles, with no attempt to turn the hips or the chest back to parallel to the flight line. The return of the wound up body will be accomplished by the knees and heels combined with the slow lateral hip slide. The slide will feel to direct the left arm down and out the angled white line.

Due to the lateral slide of the hips, with no feeling of any type of body turn, the swing will feel as if it is out to right field at 45 Degrees across the flight line. The left arm will feel as if it remains where it was at the top of the back swing, but the right forearm will be very active in making the clubhead catch up to the left hand. When the left arm and the rapidly catching up clubhead arrive at the ball the clubhead will be square to the line and travelling straight down it, as the hips turn.

THE FORMULA FOR POWER AND ACCURACY

Here we see the results of the slide of the spine caused by the actions of heels and knees, combined with the shortening of the right spinal erector. The feel of this shortening is as if we pull the right shoulder blade into the right hip pocket. The small arrows in the photo above show the rise and fall of the tilting hips, the top line is the bottom of the rib cage. The lower line is the top of the pelvis. The right forearm has begun the twirl, the club is in position to swing down under and up. From here the right arm straightens and the right hand throws. As the ball is struck the club shaft passes under the forearms and the twirl completes. The blade remains square through the hit, creating straight ball flight without side spin. The feeling is of a light twirl of the right forearm, as if opening a door knob, that starts right from the top of the back swing as the heels work and the hips slide. The twirl does not release the cup in the back of the right wrist or the bow of the left wrist. They release as the club swings through. As the hands approach the ball the right arm and hand release the clubhead under with the hand crank tossing actions, the club then catches the left arm just after impact and passes it just after the ball is gone. The club in passing the point of the triangle releases all of its energy into the back of the ball.

The path of the left arm (curved arrow) has been determined by the actions of the feet and knees and the lateral shift of the weight. The left hand is driven to here by the above actions, at an angle to the flight line as if in the direction of the arrow on the floor. From here the turn out of the right heel bends the arc as the hips drive the chest around. The left hand and with it the twirling club arrive at impact going straight down the target line like the Zoot Suiter pg 59-61.

The Feels Of The Body In The Downswing

As the back swing ends, the reversing of the directions begins. The weight, which is mostly on the straight right leg must immediately begin to shift forward onto the straightening left leg. The straightening action of the leg will thus drive the left shoulder up and this will cause the left arm to swing from the top of the back swing and pass the address hand position even though the left arm is still pinned to the chest exactly as it was at the end of the back swing.

Remember the left arm remains pinned to the chest until well after the hit. This cannot happen unless the right heel raises, the right knee flexes and the right side of the body shortens. To assist this the back muscles on the right side of the lower back must contract, the feeling is to pull the right shoulder blade into the right hip pocket. These muscles do the bulk of the work, they are assisted by the internal core muscles of the abdomen and stomach. Even though the body uses the core muscles of the obliques and the abdominals, they will never be felt as if working hard.

The body must begin to slightly arch and the belly must feel as if it goes up under the left arm. The right knee must feel as if it is lifted by the belly muscles. The right calf muscle, as the right heel lifts and turns makes the right leg run around the post of the left leg.

The head must remain in place, as if looking at the spot where the ball was, until the club has completed the release. The eyes however may follow the ball so long as the head does not turn with them. Done correctly the player should never lose sight of the ball. By doing this in just this way we guarantee a solid hit through the ball. The arms, hands and wrists will be able to fully apply their power due to the upper end of the spine being anchored in place by the still head.

After the ball has been hit and the clubhead has fully released there is no reason not to move the head and so the body simply stands up. By doing this the swing never feels to attain the bent backward look of the old style reverse "C" golf swing, but it gains its benefits. If the player does not stand up as the swing passes through this point great strain will be placed on the back unnecessarily. At the finish of the swing the body should have rotated on top of the left leg to a position where the entire body is standing straight and erect with a very slight bow to the lower back, the weight will be 95% on the left foot with what's left of the weight all of the way up on the right toe. See lower right photo page 35.

THE FORMULA FOR POWER AND ACCURACY

The Feels Of The Arms Coming Down

Pivot down to the ball in an easy relaxed manner, as you do this give the club a start by lightly turning the right forearm bones about 1/4 of a turn. The object of this move and the feel of this light spin of the right forearm is to take the lower forearm bone (near the pinky, not the thumb) and rotate it clockwise so that at hip high the lower bone is beneath the upper bone. This is not a very large or hard rotation, it begins the throwing action of the right arm much as a sidearm baseball pitcher would begin his throw. From there continue the forearm release and the forearm unwind rotation at that speed all of the way through to the finish.

The entire right arm movement is exactly like a side arm pitcher throwing a screw ball (a pitch that curves to the right), it includes the same clockwise spin feel of the screw ball throw. The right arm elbow will rise to the height of the shoulder and the right hand exactly as if you are throwing. The lower bone of the right fore-arm must be slightly behind the upper before impact, vertically aligned with it and rotating forward of it after impact as it would as you open a door knob. The right hand must feel to toss the clubhead under and past the left arm. The right elbow will rise to the height of the left arm exactly as the right wrist throws.

Try to keep your grip from getting overly tight throughout the swing, and your arms feeling soft. Pivot smoothly down and do not rush the down swing by try-ing to make a hard body move. The arms will feel as if they are coming down at the speed that gravity brings them, when the hands approach the ball whack the ball with a hard throwing action of the straightening right arm and throw type release of the right wrist. The right hand must pass between the left hand and the ball as the ball is struck, the palm of the right hand must feel to be aligned where you want the ball to go. The right wrist must make the final throwing mo-tion and the left wrist must be relaxed enough to allow it.

This slow feeling relaxed start to the downswing move will let the forearms begin to unwind back to the address position without unloading the release or attempting to hold the cup of the right wrist to delay it. The whack will be easy to time as will be the release of the right wrist and hand as it throws through.

Swinging easily yet still producing excellent power is the secret to playing good golf, not just being a powerful ball striker. You will still be a powerful ball striker doing it this way, but you will be much more accurate. Every great player of all time has had to sacrifice some of his power to attain the accuracy necessary to be great.

The Entire Swing In Action

On the following pages the photos and captions will describe what is happening at every phase of the swing. Using these photos and posing at first in each position as the mind absorbs the information about what is happening, will enable you to soon be able to slowly move through the swing and commit the actions to feel.

In some portions of the photo series we will be only using one hand, after you know what this action trains, and how it feels, add the other hand being careful to not change the actions learned by using only the training hand. Viewing the photos using a mirror will show the opposite positions, pose and feel these as well. By doing this you will both feel as well as understand the symmetry of the perfect golf swing. The only action that is not symmetrical is the rotation of the hips that drives the shoulders.

What we want to accomplish in this session is to learn what is going on and feel it as it happens. The only way you will ever become the ball striker that is within you is to train the movements into feel. Unfortunately we must intellectualize the learning process. I want you to know what and where the body does each and every part of the movement, I want you to know exactly why you are doing everything that you are doing. But most importantly I want you to feel what all of these actions are so that when you are playing the game, you can play the game.

Understand that you will never be able to play the game if you are busy trying to make your body do all of these little pieces that eventually become your golf swing.

We put a jig saw puzzle together one piece at a time, and we must be close to it in order to do it. As the picture becomes complete we can forget about the completed sections and only focus on the parts that are not correctly assembled.

Knowing what each body part is doing will let you know what is working and what needs work. Focus on fitting the pieces together that let you complete the picture.

Once completed if you remain close to a jig saw puzzle you will always see the cut lines and the picture will never be totally clear. You must learn to step back from the puzzle far enough so that the lines disappear to truly "see" it.

Once we put the swing together we must learn to mentally "step back" and let it become absorbed into feels. Of course if something is not working address that, fix it and step away again. Sometimes finding a piece that does not complete the picture leads us to re-look at the completed puzzle where we find a forced or improperly located piece. Fix that and soon you will have a swing that works by itself.

THE FORMULA FOR POWER AND ACCURACY

Positions You Should Attain In The Back Swing

The following photo series will show the exact positions that you pass through as you swing back to the top of your back swing. The captions will explain the positions verbally and tell exactly why they are important.

Why you are here

Starting from a perfect address position makes it much easier to make a perfect back swing. Notice the lowered right shoulder to implement the right hand grip.

Why you are here

Halfway back we should have the spine pointing at the right heel, the weight shift completed, and the shaft parallel to the shoulder line. While learning, this is an ideal place to check your arm and hand and spine positions before the back swing is completed by the shoulder turn. In the photo on the right Jim is checking to see if he is in the correct position, notice that the shaft and shoulders are parallel. From here the back swing is a simple abduction of the left shoulder blade and the adduction of the right shoulder blade. The shoulders turn, the hips do not.

Halfway Back

Why you are here

In the photo on the left we see the perfect halfway back position, the club and shoulders are parallel. On the right we see that the club is not parallel with the shoulders, The right elbow is not close to the hip and due to this the club is out of position, it will be likely be out of position at the top of the back swing. Returning the club properly will then be much more difficult.

Why you are here

The top of the back swing position with the wedge may seem shorter than usual, this is for control and accuracy. The body is wound plenty tight enough, and more than enough power is available from here. For a full drive simply wind it tighter, by turning the shoulders farther. Remember to not unwind the trunk as you swing down, the lower body must remain ahead of the upper body to power

Coming Down

Why You Are Here

The back swing is complete, and the downswing is beginning. The left heel will slam down and the right heel will lift, the slide of the hips will bring the left arm down the line depicted by the angled club lying on the ground. Notice in the photo above right that the left arm and hand will swing down a straight line as this happens only if the right elbow returns close to the right hip by not moving the humerus bone forward. As seen in the photo below left, the elbow has returned close to the hip and the energy of the release will be sent straight down the target line as the hips rotate. This is visible in the photo below right.

Why You Are Here

In these 2 photos we see the hit portion of the twirl, notice that the right arm is extending and the right wrist is throwing. Notice also the timing of the right knee as it goes through impact with the hands. The turn out of the right heel in the right photo is turning the hips, and driving the left hand through the hit.

Through To The Finish

Why You Are Here

In these 2 photos we see the results of the previous actions. Notice the clubface position in the left photo, it is laid back, showing that the left wrist released by flapping. It has allowed the club to swing freely, without rotating closed. The hook is eliminated, and due to its extreme speed, the clubhead is already coming back in even though the hands have not yet completed their outward journey. The photo shows the full release of energy into the ball.

In the photo on the right we see the completed follow through position. The right arm has returned the club to a fully extended behind the back position. Notice that the left wrist is fully bent back as it has been since just after impact.

The left elbow has relaxed, flexed and continued its clockwise unwind, by doing this it simply folds and gets out of the way. The action of the left arm after the hit mirrors the action of the right arm going back. Correctly done the club will finish parallel to the shoulders. Notice the full cup at the back of the left wrist.

Notice that in the photo on the left Jim has stayed down until the right shoulder has hit the chin. This very important action gives solid impact and makes the right shoulder pull the head around, In the right photo the right shoulder can be seen still touching the chin, showing he stayed down through the hit. The position of the spine shows that he has simply stood up after the release completed, thus not putting any strain on the back. At the end of the finish you should not be able to turn your head to the right. The head should be fully turned right and held from turning farther right be cause the chin is tight to the right shoulder.

THE FORMULA FOR POWER AND ACCURACY

The Swing Of The Arms And the Perfect Motion

The arms remain to the right of the body until they are brought to the ball by the pivot, The right arm twirls, straightens and throws the clubhead past the left arm as the left arm guides and controls the clubface for squareness. The ball is struck alongside or slightly in front of the right hip (depending on body type and flexibility), after impact the arms swing forward from the shoulder sockets. The right arm extends and controls the after impact arc, in exactly the reverse of the way the left arm controlled the arc in the back swing. As the ball is impacted the relaxed left arm begins to flex and fold. The left upper arm bone (Humerus) swings out from the shoulder socket and gets out of the way. By relaxing the left arm during and after impact and continuing to unwind the forearms after the hit the left arm simply folds into the arc of the straightening right arm.

The entire golf swing, until impact happens behind the player. Just as in bowling the right arm never passes the body until the ball is gone (past the foul line). It then extends fully and remains straight through the release arc.

After impact the left side of the triangle must collapse so the right arm can assume the job of creating the constant radius of the hands as they travel around the swing circle center. The triangle thus controls the size and location of the entire swinging and rotating lever assembly of the club, arms and shoulders.

Since at least 1 arm is always straight and the arms never change length the hand arc is precisely controlled. Since the swing circle center does not move, the hand arc is constant, the club always remains on plane. Combining this with the non rollover of the forearms that keeps the clubface square, as the wrist axles release, makes square and solid impact easy to obtain.

Since the hands and arms never raise the club vertically, either by raising the thumbs or lifting it with the deltoid muscles, as the tilting and rotating spine controls the tip of the triangle the perfect single plane is created.

Since the down swing plane and path are done by the weight shift and pivot the entire golf swing is controlled by correctly doing a few simple actions.

The Twirl, With No Attempt To Pull

Since the actions of the legs return the triangle any pulling action creates lineal club motion, something we do not want in this type of swing. There is a pull provided by the lateral slide and rotation of the hips, but there must be none provided by an unwinding of the chest trying to catch the hips. Any unwinding disconnects the legs as a power source, and causes the trunk muscles to assume the job putting immense strain on the vertebra and causing back trouble sooner or later. The chest must remain wound tightly to the right of the hips, this keeps the slack out between the front car (the hips) and the rear car (the chest).

There also must be no pull from the left shoulder, the left arm must be driven by the rotation of the chest, not the small muscles of the upper back. The correct feeling of all of this non pulling action is; the back must feel to stay turned to the right (the back remains feeling like it's facing the target), the left arm remains pressed to the chest. The hips first feel to slide left on a line 45 degrees to the right of the target as the feet, knees and hip tilt work. The reversing of the knees and the action of the right heel as it rises and rotates out toward the flight line then blend the shift into a rotation. This entire action controls the plane, the path and supplies the needed power to hit the ball long and straight.

The twirl of the clubhead done by the unwind of the wound up forearms provide much rotational speed to the club around the wrists at the apex of the arm shoulder triangle. As the triangle re forms, due to the straightening right arm, and releasing flap of the hands, gravity and centrifugal force help increase the speed of the free swinging clubhead.

The twirl of the clubhead continues, as the left elbow relaxes and flexes to complete the arm swing action. The upper body continues to rotate once the hips have turned as far as they can go, it now unwinds and the right shoulder follows the right hand as the straight right arm now controls the arc of the clubhead.

The actions, as above described, allow the hands and forearms to twirl the clubhead in time with the rotation of the body, on the proper inside out plane and path. The free releasing wrists as the flap cause the clubhead to be square throughout the entire hitting zone. The player may sometimes push or pull the shot if the heel and knee timing gets out of whack, with the timing of the twirl, but due to the wrist flap hand release, rather than the common release with rolling forearms, the ball still flies straight although a bit off line, with little to no curvature. A far better outcome than a slice, hook or a combination of those with a push or a pull. You may actually miss the shot but still hit the green a lot.

Controlling The Down Swing Path And Plane

If you hit the ball left of your intended target without curvature you have an out to in swing path and you must adjust your downswing path. There are several ways of doing this, first make sure that you are shifting your weight on to the left foot and straight left leg by replanting your left heel and lifting your right heel as you start down. To do this **pull** the left knee straight back under the left hip, **remember to flex the right knee and lift the right heel at the same time**, **do not attempt to turn the hips or the chest**. This will make the hips slide laterally left, you should feel your belly go up under your left arm. You will feel as if you are slightly arching your back. As you do this bunch up the muscles in your right lower back and try to pull the right side of your rib cage close to the top of your right hip. Feeling as if you are pulling the right shoulder blade into the right hip pocket is a good mental picture. To get the feeling swing easily.

Your body will move as if you are trying to bump someone standing to your left, hard enough to move him a few feet, with your left hip. As the left leg gets straight the lifting right heel then rotates out toward the flight line and provides the turning action of the pelvis on top of the now posted up left leg.

Correctly done the path will be perfect, and consistent practice of this while learning it will soon make it a habit. This move is critical, and it must be grooved by not doing it wrong for 30 days. Once you have done it perfectly every day for those 30 days it will be as easy and natural to do as breathing.

To perfect this critical part of the swing we must not even once do it wrong. To this end I would suggest that for those 30 days you never swing harder than 75% of the distance that you usually get with your normal golf swing. If you make an error during this training period, remember that you must re-start your 30 days from that swing forward. If you attempt to rip at the ball during the training period you will invariably make errors, and increase your frustration by grooving the errors, thus making learning difficult at best, and potentially impossible. You must get the feeling of the force, you cannot force the feeling.

This 75% swing when done properly will give you roughly the same distance you had with your old full swing anyway, thus you can play as you learn. Do not forget to start down slowly as you shift, and then feel to increase club speed.

With patience, discipline and persistence you will within months have a golf swing that stands up under any kind of pressure and delivers accurate, powerful and precisely controlled golf shots. You will have arrived.

The Swing of the Unimpeded Clubhead

For the golf club to impart its energy into the ball with as much as possible of its energy going into the ball, the concept of hitting the ball with the clubhead passing the hands is very important. The clubhead must strike the ball just before the entire club actually catches the in line condition with the left arm. I have heard and seen much about getting the clubhead to the ball too soon, words like the clubhead never passes the hands etc. The condition of the clubhead getting in front of the hands is so unusual, that it is extremely unlikely that it is yours or for that matter anyone else's problem. Generally players tend to not allow the clubhead to fully release, most players hold on to the release. By not allowing the club to swing and hit the ball, they end up with the clubhead trailing the hands. Doing this makes the bulk of the release happen after the ball is gone. I often tell my students, who are pivoting properly, to try to get the clubhead to the ball before the hands get there. As of this date, none have managed to do it. To help visualize what you want to happen as the ball is struck, the sketches on the following pages give a good mental picture. Done this way the clubhead during impact will be carrying much speed and due to the full release it will still be accelerating.

You must fully release the clubhead for full power and ball flight control. For this to happen our grip must be light enough, our forearms must be still twirling, our right triceps and wrist extension must be completing the throwing motion by straightening the right arm. As the clubhead travels through the area where it strikes the ball the right hand throw of the release must also be occurring. These actions require the free flap if the left wrist to happen. If the left wrist does not flap to allow the right hand to pass between the clubhead and the ball, the right hand cannot hit through. If you lock the wrist the crank release will not happen and the pendulum will not swing through the hit. Also if the left elbow does not relax and fold down through the hit the right arm cannot create the conical action of the correct follow through. The feeling for the left arm is a palm down at first (just after the hit) to a relaxed, cop saying stop position (see photo page 135) as the release finishes. When the pendulum swings freely, like this, much more energy is imparted to the ball, distance is then created by clubhead speed, not brute force.

The sketches on the next pages show the club fully catching up to the left arm, contact however must be made slightly before the complete catch up happens, and the release must continue through impact. You must have the club still accelerating as you hit, after straight the club begins to slow down, and that condition greatly reduces distance.

The Full Release

The Hit Through

The photo above left shows the left wrist and forearm positions as the club approaches the ball, notice the bowed wrist as used by Ben Hogan. Mr. Hogan said that the wrist was in this position at impact, I can't find anything he wrote that said it was locked in this position, I believe he let it release. The photo below left, shows the final release of the bow as the right hand hits through.

When the wrists release this way it is so fast that it cannot be seen by the naked eye. The release of this bowed position creates much accuracy. Once the desired impact alignments are set at address simply swing and hit through as usual. There is no need to try to force curvature or height control the alignments do it.

The photos above show how the right hand can accelerate the clubhead past the left arm. The job of the right arm is to throw the clubhead around the outside of the arc, like a ball around a maypole, and past the left arm through the hit. It must be very active, since it is the true producer of clubhead speed. Above right the forearms almost touch as the left wrist flexes and the right arm extends.

Note that the left elbow (lower left photo) is already beginning to fold, this duplicates, in reverse, the actions of the right arm in the back swing. The folding arm collapses into the arc created by the straight arm. Relax the left arm, let the elbow fold, and the armpit open as the humerus swings out (mirror the pic on pg 144). The right arm, as it crosses the chest, will put it into the perfect positions.

Passing The Point

For this swing to properly function it is important to hit the ball with the speeding and free releasing clubhead, not the whole club as if to push the ball with the shaft. The feel is much like twirling the key ring, you cannot push the keys faster with the chain, you must twirl them to make speed.

To do this it is vital to make the clubhead travel much faster than the approaching left hand and arm. We do this with the right arm motion that is a combination of twirling and throwing. Twirling builds early speed by using the unwind of the forearm muscles, throwing adds the use of the entire right arm.

As a child, you probably have thrown a ball around a maypole, and so understand that a throw of a tethered object rotates it in a rapid motion around a fixed point. When gravity helps it is even faster.

In this swing, the left wrist axle is the fixed point (the point of the triangle), but this point is being brought in an arc around the swing circle center very rapidly by the pivot. As we swing we want to throw the clubhead around this point so that it catches up to and passes the point of the triangle, this way we will reach full extension with maximum speed. The left arm acts as a guide, and the release of the hinging wrist allows only a square clubface through impact.

To learn how to do this it is important to first feel this action by doing it very slowly. We will learn to feel this by using a sand wedge, and only making a half swing, We use a sand wedge because it has a short shaft and a very heavy clubhead, This makes it easy to feel. It is the feel of doing this correctly that we must cultivate as we swing faster and use the longer, lighter clubs.

Make a slow short (about 1/2 swing) downswing, and with a rapid twirling action, twirl / throw the clubhead past the left hand while being sure to keep the back of the left hand facing the target during the time that the clubhead swings through the wrist axle release area. Make absolutely sure that the right hand passes between the left hand and the ball through impact. The ease of making power and the height and distance of the resulting shot may surprise you.

Gradually increase the size of the back swing, hold the # 7 position, keep the shoulders wound behind (to the right of) the hips. Slam down the left heel, pick up the right heel and knee, arch the back, feel like you are pulling the right shoulder into the right hip pocket and throw the clubhead through the ball and past the left hand. Remember to go slowly, you must learn to walk before you run.

Putting Back What You Took Out

As you swing the club back to the top of the back swing you create several angles between the clubhead and the left arm. The first of these angles is the sideward wrist cock which retracts the club 45 degrees to the right of the point of the arm shoulder triangle. Next comes the folding action of the right arm at the elbow which gives 45 more degrees of travel. The sketches depict this action far better than words.

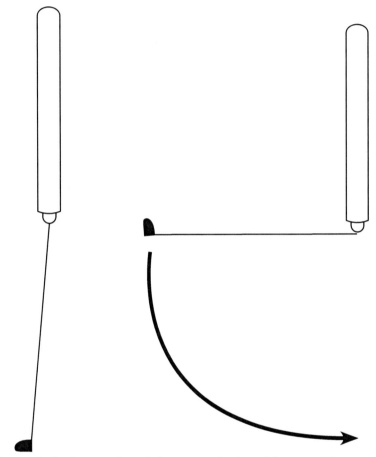

The sketch above left shows the club arm relationship at address, they are nearly in line. The sketch above right shows the club cocked 90 degrees behind the right arm, this is a combination of the wrist set and the right arms flex at the elbow. From here the right hand and arm could propel the ball quite a long way simply by straightening out the lever.

If we stopped halfway back in the back swing (halfway back is when the left arm is just short of parallel to the ground, sketch facing page) we would have rotated the left arm 90 degrees away from the ball. The clubhead, due to the previously described actions would be 90 degrees farther away than the left hand is. From here it is obvious that the clubhead would have to go twice as fast as the left hand to catch up, since it is twice as far from the ball (degree wise) as the left arm.

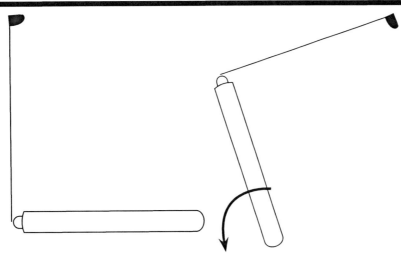

Above left we see the left arm and the club together rotated 90 degrees farther, the left arm is now 90 degrees from the ball, the club is another 90 degrees further behind the arm, the clubhead is now 180 degrees away from the ball. Above right we see that the left arm has been rotated back an additional 80 degrees or so (some players can rotate it even farther). From here the clubhead must be swung at twice the speed of the left hand in order to catch up to the left hand, which itself is being driven quickly around in the direction of the black arrow by the weight shift and pivot. The clubhead must be twirled hard and fully released for it to catch up to and pass the left hand through impact. Ideally we return to almost the same left arm club relationship we established at address.

Since the pivot returns the top end of the club quickly and powerfully as the weight shift and leg action returns the left arm, the right hand must be very active to get the clubhead around in time for the club ball collision. For powerful and accurate shots the right hand must start twirling exactly as the legs start bringing the triangle down, to make the clubhead catch up to the left arm. Thus they are starting the hit right at the top of the back swing.

Again I repeat the right hand will start twirling the clubhead at the ball at exactly the same instant that the heels and knees start to do their actions, this gives the clubhead much speed as it comes around in a broad arc, The club and arm will act as if they were a long lever swung from the swing circle center as they strike the ball. This is much better then a short lever the length of the club swinging from the wrist. However since the clubhead is travelling much faster than the whole lever, as the wrists flap sideways, the impact on the ball is as if the whole lever were traveling at that speed. The broad down swing arc places a strong drag on the left arm, that is why the maintenance of the trunk wind and late turn of the hips is so dynamic, the legs will have hit the ball by driving the left arm and to this we add the speed given the clubhead by the right hand twirl.

THE FORMULA FOR POWER AND ACCURACY

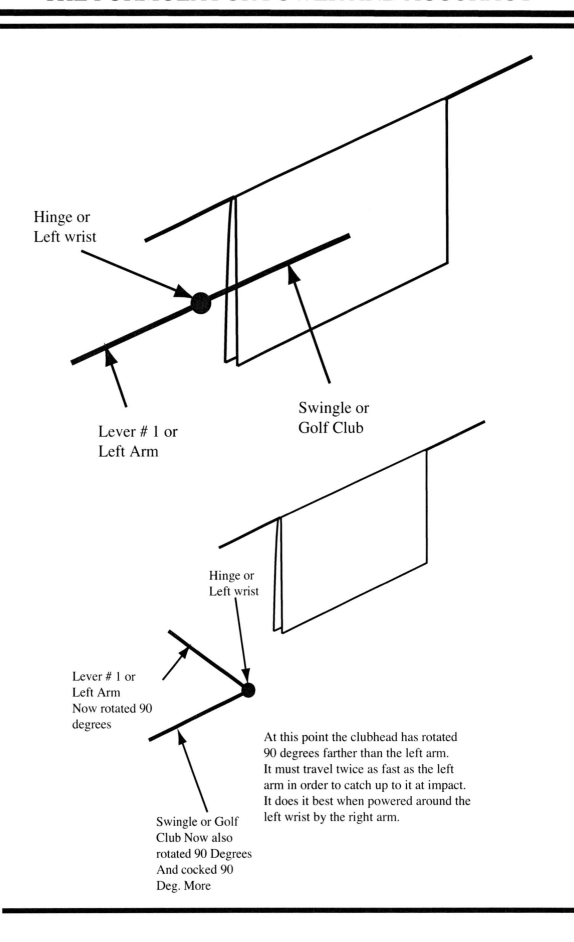

Hinge or
Left wrist

Swingle or
Golf Club

Lever # 1 or
Left Arm

Hinge or
Left wrist

Lever # 1 or
Left Arm
Now rotated 90
degrees

Swingle or Golf
Club Now also
rotated 90 Degrees
And cocked 90
Deg. More

At this point the clubhead has rotated
90 degrees farther than the left arm.
It must travel twice as fast as the left
arm in order to catch up to it at impact.
It does it best when powered around the
left wrist by the right arm.

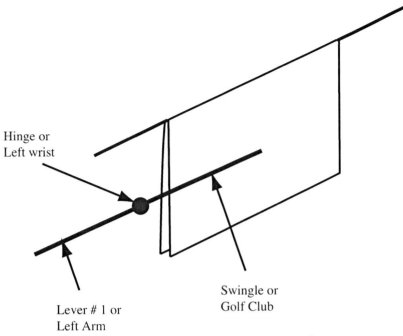

Hinge or
Left wrist

Lever # 1 or
Left Arm

Swingle or
Golf Club

For the Club to return to this position it must travel twice as fast as the returning left arm
The Club must catch up to the left arm to have a full release, it must freely   ·
swing past it without being impeded to release all of its energy into the ball.

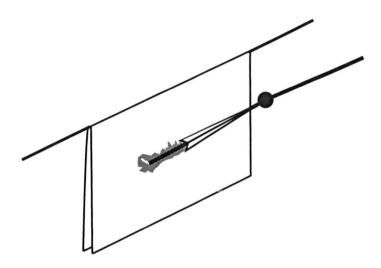

Seen from the other side, we must envision the swingle
tearing through the carpet with the end emerging first
and the carpet ripping back toward the hands as the speeding
clubhead gets way out in front of the hands. The swinging of
the golf club through the ball must feel this way. It must pass
the hands not just catch up to it.
When this feeling is attained, the clubhead advances through the
hit. This is the ultimate release of energy into the ball and gives
much distance to the shot. The right arm has released its whack.

Trajectory and Curvature

Trajectory And Curvature Control

As you have learned the clubface is not revolving around the shaft as it passes through the impact area, but rather coming from de-lofted to whatever loft you choose to use; it then gets increased loft as the wrists flap and the hands release the club through the bottom of the cone. Due to this action the clubface remains, as set at address relative to the ball, throughout a large potential impact area. To hit a shot with curvature requires only that we set the clubface open or closed relative to the flight line before we take our grip. See photos pages 176-177.

To control the trajectory we move the ball forward and back on the flight line. Forward produces higher shots, rearward produces lower shots.

As we move the ball forward and back we must keep the clubface square to the flight line by not taking our grip until after the club is positioned as to shaft lead angle and face direction.

Taking our stance, it is vital to keep the butt end of the club pointing at a spot just right of the left hip, thus the shaft will be leaning toward the target for low shots and closer to vertical for higher shots. Remember that the shaft must have some forward (toward the target) lean angle to produce the downward blow necessary to keep from hitting fat or scooping the shot.

Due to the down under and up release we use rather than the out over and around actions of the standard release, the range of ball placement with this swing is quite amazing to those who have been using the standard swing. The standard swing requires the ball to be in a particular spot for solid contact to even be possible. If the ball is moved forward or back squaring the club at impact becomes very difficult.

With this swing we can play the ball as far forward as a not quite vertical shaft angle at address, to a position 6 or more inches to the right of the right foot. When the ball is played this far back it is possible to hit a 7 iron under a card table 100 yards out. The ability to hit low stinger type shots is extremely valuable for escaping from trouble by going under branches etc. or playing into the wind. When the ball is placed far back in the stance the ground will stop the club quickly, since the downward angle is so steep that the divot would be very deep, in some cases so deep that it would be impossible for the club to dig out that much turf. Be careful not to hurt your self by swinging down and trying to fully release the hands in the swing while hitting these type low shots. Simply smack the ball and then let the earth stop the club, do not try to dig a deep ditch.

Lower Than Normal Shots

Due to the conical arc of the releasing clubhead controlling trajectory is a simple matter of ball placement. This is done when taking the stance, simply create a different loft than normal, by leaning the shaft farther forward than the normal lead angle. When doing this remember to also position the clubface square to the flight line, and position your body so that the shaft and your left arm are a straight line (seen from face on). To do this the entire body must move left, feet and all. The ball will then be much farther to the right than normal. The ball can be played as much as 6 inches or more to the right of your right foot on a wedge. The ball on low flying shots will always be to the right of your head at address. Swinging down do not allow your head to move right, if you do you will cancel the loft change and hit the ball higher than you want, since the swing circle center is now located farther right. The head must remain as at address.

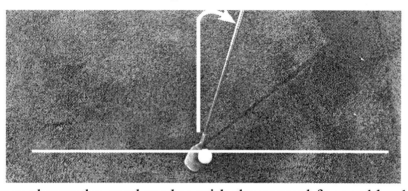

The photo above shows the sand wedge with the normal forward lead angle, the ball would be directly in the center of the stance and the shot would have the normal launch angle. The fat white line indicates vertical. Notice that the shaft leans toward the target and the blade is square to the flight line.

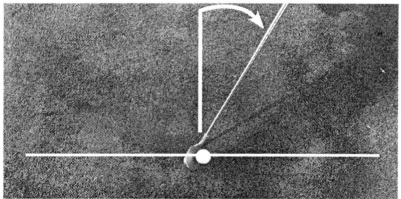

This photo shows the ball well back in the stance for a lower flying shot. The shaft leans much farther forward from vertical. The leading edge of the club must remain square, do this before you take your grip. The ball will fly lower with good backspin but will bounce forward before the spin takes.

Higher than Normal Shots

Hitting higher than normal shots can be done two ways, the first is a reverse of the low shot set-up. Simply position the ball farther forward in the stance and reduce the normal lead angle, this increases the loft. It is important to not that you cannot go beyond vertical with the shaft (except in a bunker), or you will hit a fat shot, due to the bottom of the release arc occurring behind the ball. I suggest that you always have some forward lean for insurance against this.

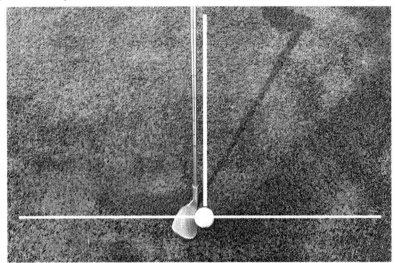

This photo shows the maximum amount of vertical shaft angle, this removes any downward motion to the clubhead at impact, it is a dangerous shot and must only be attempted from a fluffy lie with the ball perched as if on a tee.

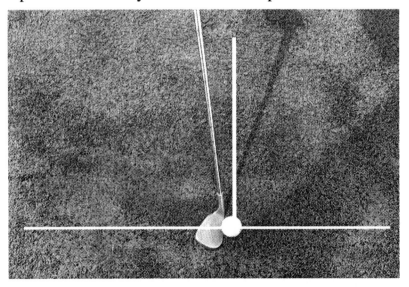

This shaft angle virtually guarantees a fat shot, its only use is in rare instances in a bunker when extra height is a must. It is easier to get extra height by opening the clubface by rotating the shaft and face open before taking the grip. It should only be used when simply opening the face still does not give enough

Another Way

The second way to hit the shot higher than normal is to open the clubface by twisting the shaft so that the face rotates clockwise, this opens the leading edge of the clubface to the flight line and increases loft. This is illustrated in the photo below. It will produce higher ball flight on the shorter shots, but will induce some side spin and the bounce of the ball will move it right on landing. On longer shots the ball will curve right and also bounce right. The curve in flight does not need to be compensated for on shorter shots since the ball is not spinning fast enough or flying long enough for curvature to occur. The bounce to the right does need compensation, since we are normally trying to hole these shots or land the ball on an exact spot to take advantage of the slope of the green.

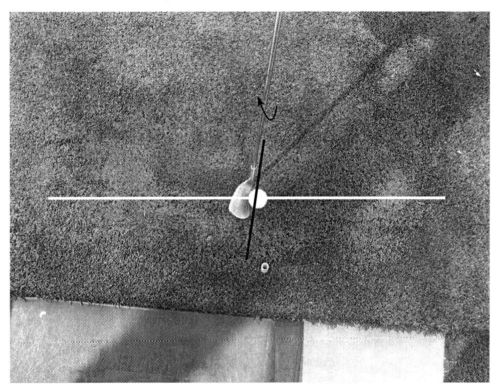

The clubface can be seen rotated open in the photo above, the lead angle of the shaft is normal. The blade can thus be rotated to increase the loft without changing the lead angle, this does however put some side spin on the ball. You can by using a combination of shaft rotation and lead angle variation produce varying lofts as well as attack angles. This gives the ability to hit the ball higher than normal (open clubface) and still have a downward blow (forward lead angle). Thus we can cut the ball up with some spin if we desire by hitting down with the decreased lead angle or lob it up with little spin (on the shorter shots) with less lead angle. On longer shots with less lead angle and high clubhead speeds more spin may be induced depending on clubface ball impact conditions.

Drawing The Ball

The ability to curve the ball at will and do it in a controlled fashion is another of the advantages of the conical release. Since the clubface alignments do not change throughout a large part of the swing and not at all through the impact area whatever face alignments we choose to set at address remain through impact. This means that when we address the ball we can set the exact impact alignments we want the clubface to have at impact, before completing the left hand grip, and then simply swing the club normally with no other changes to the swing and get the shot that we expect.

The function of the machine never changes, we change the tool and we change the alignments of the tool at address and from that point on we simply make the golf swing. For this to happen we need to know what the impact alignment for each desired shot looks like, the photo below shows the impact alignment to produce right to left curvature. For a draw the toe of the club is ahead of the heel at impact, thus hitting outside a straight line drawn through the center of the ball. Naturally how much curvature depends on how radically we set it. The hardest part of hitting the shot is the making of a normal swing once the alignments are changed. It is easy to try to help the club produce curvature or hold on and thus prevent it. Some time practicing these will pay handsome dividends in actual play.

Never hit a shot in competition that you cannot hit at least 9 times out of ten at the range. The bad shot should never happen on the first of these, since the first shot in play is the only one that matters. You should also be aware of what your tendencies are for the misses. You need to know where your miss will end up,

 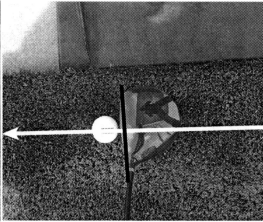

For a straight shot the face is 90 degrees to the flight line.

For a draw the toe hits first. For both shots the clubhead is traveling straight down the arrow.

Fading The Ball

A fade is simply the reverse of the draw alignment, the face will be set a little open at address, for both of these shots the stance and ball position are the same as for your standard straight drive. Needless to say you must have your swing working well enough to be able to hit the ball reasonably straight. If you cannot, something is wrong in your execution of the swing, since the shot should fly straight with little or no curvature when the swing is working right. Find the error, and repair it. To hit the controlled fade simply open the clubface by rotating the shaft a few degrees clockwise before applying your left hand grip. As you learn this you will realize just how little or much curvature you get with the adjustments. You will also be learning how this also affects trajectory.

If you find that it is easy to curve the ball right or more difficult to draw the ball it is likely that you have not trained your self to fully release the clubhead through impact. Go back to the range and work on that release, when you can draw or fade the driver and are sure that it is going to happen and that if it doesn't draw or fade when you want it to that the worst it would do is go straight you have a big advantage over your competitors. Naturally you will find it much easier to work your irons, until you start trying to draw and fade the short irons. Since the short irons produce much more backspin than side spin these short clubs require extra adjustment angles, plus a hard forearm roll over to produce a draw (forget a slice, it cant be done). Do not attempt to put a large curve on these clubs in play, unless you are playing match play and not doing it results in a loss of hole anyway. What you can use the slight curvature for is to bounce the ball in the direction of the curvature after impact. It is often easier to affect the ground curvature than the flight curvature with these short clubs.

If the clubface follows the white arrow the shot is an intentional fade, Notice that the clubface hits the inside rear quadrant of the ball. The toe lags behind.

If you intend to swing down the white arrow to get a small fade, but unintentionally swing down the black arrow you will get a slice. The face alignment is the same but the path increases the spin.

This is the impact alignment that produces left to right curvature, the intentional fade. If your ball curves to the right, when you try to hit it straight, this may be what your clubface looks like at impact. Try releasing the right hand harder, or slowing down the left arm so that the right hand can hit through. An undesired fade or slice could also indicate a path error. The blade alignment can be square or even slightly shut, but the clubhead path may follow the black arrow rather than the white one, causing side spin and curvature to the right.

Combining Curvature And Trajectory

To hit shots with varying amounts of curvature, it is a simple matter of combining the two factors that create curvature and trajectory. Shaft angle (lead angle) creates face impact loft angle, Clubface angle (caused by rolling the shaft open or closed before finalizing the grip) controls face impact alignments. Assuming that the club is following the straight down the flight line path and releasing fully with the conical release whatever alignments you set at address will return at impact. The shots will be very predictable if the swing remains the same.

The only way to become adept at using these adjustments is to practice creating these shots. Start by just hitting perfectly straight shots with a 7 iron, and once the swing is working well open or close the face a tiny amount and watch the ball flight closely for curvature. Be certain that you are fully releasing in the conical manner. Gradually increase the angle of the clubface by opening or closing the clubface before gripping, you will soon be hitting shots that curve as desired and you will be able to see how much open or closed the face needs to be to curve the ball the desired amount. Now vary the lead angle to control the vertical launch angle, then blend the two. Use only the 7 iron for the first few practice sessions. When you can predict the flight of the ball and then create the alignments that make it happen use the 8 iron and the 6 iron and practice the same thing. You are stocking your mental bank with the understanding of what combining these alignments does.

Go up all of the way to the driver and you will have mastered basic curvature control. Once this is mastered, try all of these things from an open stance to see what happens with an out to in clubhead path and with a closed stance for the in to out path. To open the stance, starting from the normal stance, move your left foot 1 inch closer to the flight line and your right foot 1 inch farther from it. This will rotate you without moving the swing circle center opening the stance. Bigger adjustments or closed stance adjustments are done similarly. The ball will move forward in the stance when it is closed and back when it is open.

You must then make sure that your clubface is square to the flight line, not to your shoulder line. From the open stance, the shot will start straight but higher and it will curve to the right. You will find that the closed stance will move the ball forward giving a closed clubface and clubhead at address and impact. This stance adjustment produces a lower flying draw. Naturally, in play, you will make the necessary aim adjustments to give room for the curve. First learn how much curve and launch angle the adjustments give in practice before using them in play. Start with small changes. No one can do this for you. You must experiment in practice.

Diagnosing And Repairing The Error

When we combine lead angle and clubface angle the equation becomes more difficult. We start running into two of the most difficult to hit shots in the game, the low slice, and the high hook. Since the hook flies lower than normal and the fade flies higher than normal the adjustments of lead angle and face alignment must work together to produce these shots. Before we discuss how to hit these two beauties, that we hope we never have to hit but that if pulled off often demoralize an opponent, let me re-phrase their names. The hook is nothing more than an extreme draw, and the slice is a huge fade. We know that either the open clubface or an out to in clubhead path create the fade, and that the opposite produces the draw with our release. If that is the case then these unwanted shots, should you hit one unintentionally tell you that either the clubface was too closed (draw), or too open (fade), assuming that the path was correct. If the path was wrong, the face alignments may also have been wrong.

The first step is to diagnose the error, find a place were a few divots wont matter (like your own lawn). Make a swing with your 6 iron and look at the divot, with our release the ends should be square and the divot should look like a dollar bill. If the ends are angled you are rolling the club over and the conical release needs work. Next, try to make a swing that would put a divot right alongside, and in the same exact direction of the first divot but with an inch or two of grass between them. Examine the second divot. Are they parallel? Or does the second divot either angle away from or toward the first divot. The second divot tells the tale, it will tell you if your swing path is correct or if it goes in a different direction. If the divot angles left make sure that you are shifting the weight before turning with a cross line out to right field feeling. If the divot angles right look to the turn out of the right foot through impact, it is likely late.

If the divot goes straight with square ends your ball has to fly straight, unless you are not swinging the clubhead past the left hand due to impeding the pendulum by not allowing the clubhead to swing.

To hit a high hook play the ball forward in a closed stance, position the shaft as vertically as you dare, but keep a bit of lead angle. Shut the face as much as you dare, make sure to shift your weight and shorten the lower right back muscle. Swing through and try to hit up and out on the ball. To hit the low slice reverse these alignments. Ball back, open stance, much lead angle, and an open clubface. Swing normally. The clubface must remain open through the hit. These shots require much practice. Never hit these shots in play unless absolutely forced to. But learn how to do them in practice, they will make the other shots easier to do.

THE FORMULA FOR POWER AND ACCURACY

Random Thoughts That May Help

This swing slightly differs from the Kill the Ball, long driving contest swing, by using a less violent lateral movement. The hip slide although less pronounced still creates much leverage and the shots will still be very powerful. By reducing the width of the slide we give ourselves a far better chance of creating the solid centered contact so necessary for competitive play rather than the maximum power output of the long driving contest swing,

The arms swing, after impact, as freely as if they were 2 ropes attached to the shoulders, however they will not swing from the shoulder sockets until after the ball is struck. The arc of the swing will feel to be very large in front of the ball, and the hand release will feel to be total.

The twirl of the hands must retain the right wrist in the bent back position until the right elbow has rotated around and approaches the right hip, when this happens we will be able to unload fully through the ball at exactly the right point in the swing to make use of the hip turn and all of our arm power and speed at exactly the right spot in the action.

The unwinding of the forearms occurs naturally if the arms and shoulders are allowed to totally relax and be swung down by the weight shift, and later whipped around by the turn of the hips. Waiting to slap with the right wrist until the hands are passing through the ball will allow the maximum build up of speed through the hit with a minimum expenditure of physical effort.

The arms will unwind and the wrists will un-cock (in their flapping manner) at exactly the right spot and with the clubface square so long as the dues of practice has been paid in the short pitch shot drills.

The 50 yard sand wedge shot contains all of the movements of a full 1 iron or driver, but these movements are being done at a manageable speed so that the timing and feel of the swing and the release point can be felt and grooved.

The short pitch shot is the key to fine golf, if you become proficient at the 60 yard and under pitch shot, you will have a much lower bogey percentage. You will find yourself able to get up and down much more often and your scores will plummet. Being a good pitcher of the ball takes much pressure off the putter and gives great confidence as to ones ability to shoot low scores.

Impact

Everything we do in the golf swing is directed toward only one goal. It is the application of the clubhead to the ball, as we impart our minds energy into the ball to create its desired actions. This is the moment of truth, at impact the alignments of the clubface as to angle of attack, squareness of contact and path create a message that the ball will respond to perfectly. The ball will only do what we tell it to do and it will fly exactly the way the input we gave it dictates unless it is influenced by outside factors such as a collision with a tree or a reaction to wind etc. When struck, the ball does exactly what the impact alignments tell it to do, good alignments, good shot. Bad alignments, bad shot. Correct amount of power applied, correct distance, incorrect power etc.

Of course this is assuming that the clubface is dry and has no grass between it and the ball. In those situations the outcome of the shot can be very unpredictable.

To create the shot that we desire we naturally must have the proper alignments for the shot shape desired, and the proper ball placement for trajectory control. These things we deal with as we take our address and our grip. In all but the rarest instances we will make our normal golf swing, since the swing movements do not change from club to club. Only when trying for extreme curvature or in avoiding an obstacle such as a tree in our swing path do we make a modification to our basic movements. Just as a drill press does not change its basic motion to drill a large hole or a smaller one we simply change the tool (club) and the power applied to it. The basic motion of the drill press remains the same just as our basic swing motions remain the same.

Correct Club Weighting And Shaft Fitting

For the golf shot to have its maximum potential, we must have the application of the releasing energy creating a situation where at impact the clubhead is approaching or at maximum velocity. The clubhead must either be accelerating or at maximum velocity at impact. Generally we want to strike the ball just before maximum velocity to guarantee that the club is accelerating rather than decelerating. When the clubhead is still accelerating the shaft will still have some flex so that it can add its kick through impact, rather than have impact potentially decelerating a free flying clubhead. Continued on the next page.

THE FORMULA FOR POWER AND ACCURACY

We can only have one instant of maximum acceleration as we approach maximum speed, it must occur through the hit for peak effectiveness. Even though we begin to accelerate the clubhead right from the top of the downswing we do not release the final expenditure of the clubs energy until the weight shift has brought the hands almost all of the way back to the ball. The full release of the right hand as it passes under the left wrist axle must be timed to occur with the hip rotation and the right foot's action of rotating the knee, and hip by getting up on to the tip of the toe. This action can be seen and felt as having the hit occur as the right knee and hands arrive at and pass the ball.

When properly done the clubhead will be behind the arc of the bent shaft at impact, it will then be supported by a pre bent shaft which will then have a greater resistance to kickback and which also can add a boost to the release as the shaft kicks while the ball is on the clubface. The clubhead would thus be supported by the shaft and not be simply having the energy of its own weight and speed.

To create a driver that kicks at exactly the correct instant for this type swing the players hit style must be known to the club fitter, since this release action stresses the shaft in a different manner and at a different time in the swing. The shaft flex and kick point as well as the balance of clubhead weight are all factors that must be considered. These factors are further weighted by the players swing speed potential. Generally the off the rack drivers and the common fitting method produces drivers that are too light for this method. Within reason this is similar to saying I can drive a large nail easier, and with less effort, with a heavy hammer than I can with a light hammer. The heavier driver requires a different type of balance, to make it still feel easy to swing. These drivers are available at a surprisingly low price. A properly fitted driver for this swing method can create more powerful drives and at the same time feel easier to swing. See the web site for ordering details.

Since most better players use steel shafts in the irons, these clubs require less precision as to shaft torque, steel shafts are recommended for this swing method in the irons for accuracy. If you feel you must have graphite shafts, perhaps to lessen impact shock, they should be high end shafts with very low torque.

Shaft flex with this swing can be extremely stiff or even soft so long as the torque is low. Generally softer shafts produce higher ball flight, although very strong players will over torque the softer shafts when their hand strength adds the bend of flex to the twist of torque, causing erratic impact alignments.

Bringing The Game To The Course

How do we use all of these mental pictures to create the perfect golf swing?

One cannot attempt to play using the images I have worked so hard to give you through the text and sketches in this book. They are only given to help you get a mind picture of how we do what we do, and to get you feeling how it feels to do it right. Since golf is played almost entirely by feel, it stands to reason that the more feel we develop, the better a player we will become.

The basic way of developing these feels is to train each body part, hands, feet etc. to do their actions individually, first through the movement drills and later through the shot drills that train each body part. As these become mastered we must join them with the other body actions, then and only then will the overall swing improve.

Many players while learning the individual body part actions become so focused on these individual actions that it does detriment to the whole. It is the root of much frustration to be able to do the drills correctly but to not be able to put the whole thing together in practice or to bring the swing to the course when we play.

To get beyond this requires that we have a different set of thoughts when we are making the entire golf swing versus when we are training the body how to do it.

WE CAN BECOME SO INVOLVED IN HOW WE DO WHAT WE ARE DOING, THAT BY DOING SO WE LOSE OUR FOCUS ON WHAT IT <u>IS</u> THAT WE ARE DOING.

In practice when working on the complete swing, be the shot long or short, as in playing the game, we must focus on <u>what we want the ball to do.</u> Rather than what we want our bodies to do, to make the ball do what we want it to do.

It is the learning in our practice sessions to let the trained actions of the body work, without conscious guidance, that gives us the control of the shot that the mind picture desires. The mind must let the body do it and not attempt to guide it by controlling the parts in their actions. In practice we must focus on the feel of a good shot and learn to recreate that feel as we swing. In play make a few practice swings to feel a good swing and then just do it. Your play will improve.

The Mental Side Of Practice And Play

In practice if we do not get the shot that we desired, we must quickly analyze the reason for what caused the error, focus on what went wrong and repeat the correct movement by practice swinging before the next similar shot. The next shot or two we should focus on making sure that the correct movement is executed, and then go back to focusing on letting the body create the shot that the mind visualizes. This practice session mind set, quickly builds confidence and touch. On the golf course we do not have the luxury of a re-do, however there is no rule that says you cannot analyze the error and make a few swings without a ball to reinforce the feel of doing it right. Just be sure to repair any divots or damage these shots may create. When the next similar shot comes up focus on the repair while doing a practice swing. Then while focusing on the shot at hand, not the repair, hit the shot. Your new success level will please you.

An ex PGA tour pro friend of mine once said, most people on the golf course are not playing golf, they are playing Golf Swing. What he meant by this is that they are so busy giving themselves a lesson as to how to do what they are doing before and during each shot that they fail to focus on simply doing the shot. This is akin to a chess player trying to read a book on how to play chess while attempting to win a chess match. If he were to divide his attention this way he would not play well and would probably lose. So it is in each and every shot we make in golf, our full focus must be on what we are doing, not how we go about doing what we are doing. See the shot in your minds eye, make a practice swing to feel it and then just do it.

Most players who have been around the game for several years have seen the guy with the funny swing who does not hit particularly spectacular shots, yet is able to scrape the ball around and, through extreme focus, shoot a winning or at least respectable score. Since their swing is faulty they must use intense focus to make it work. Generally these type players will excel in the short game, the reason for this is, those players put the same intense focus on everything that they do when close to the green. It is this extreme focus of making the ball do what ever it is that we want it to do that gets the conscious mind out of the directing the body mode, and into the playing mode. To this end we must first train the parts. We then join the parts into units, once the units are created we join the units into the whole. This is done as we practice. During play we must learn to let the sub-conscious mind direct the movements of the body as we focus solely on the desired outcome of the shot. The mind picture will then direct the machine.

The Simplest of Concepts

Once the mind understands this concept, and the motions of each of the swing parts have been learned and practiced, here is a very simple way of conceiving the golf swing; use these thoughts as you practice or make a practice swing.

Swing the club back to the top of the back swing simply by pulling the right knee, not the hip, back. As you do it tuck the left pinky, wind the forearms and turn the shoulders. Starting down, keep the chest wound right and the left arm back as you reverse the knees, pick up the right heel and twirl the club, make no effort to turn any part of the body left (especially the hips and chest).

Focus on starting the feet and the twirl of the unwinding forearms at the same time, as you send the energy cross line. Remember all of the turning action of the body is a product of the hip slide and the reversal of the knee positions, this rotation is kept moving by the turn out of the right heel. Doing this turns the hips and the retarded chest. After impact the residual energy left in the speeding clubhead pulls you to the finish.

Totally release the wrists as you return the club to in line with the left arm at impact and let the clubhead go. Make the right hand pass between the left hand and the ball and do not roll the clubface closed. Instead freely release the left wrist (let it flap) and hit through with the right hand and arm. Enjoy the shot.

This may seem like a lot of things to do and to think about at first. Soon you will find that you do some of these things well and others need to be thought of to make them happen. When you reach this stage in your learning, you can simply focus on the things that do not happen automatically.

As time goes by your goal is to simply see the flight of the ball that you want, set up, take the club back and hit the ball with it. Usually the last skills that you need to perfect is the total clubhead release and the start down in the cross line energy direction.

This will occur as you are approaching perfection, the game will be simple then since your thoughts can be; Take it back, focus on the cross line hit and totally release the club. 3 Simple thoughts each at a different point in the action, easy to do and soon also easily blended into the final concept.

Take it back, and hit the ball.

May I wish you the success you seek in your golfing future.

Dan Shauger

FOR PERSONAL INSTRUCTION, AND PRODUCTS
DESIGNED TO IMPROVE YOUR GAME CHECK THE
WEB SITE
www.aperfectswing.com

THIS BOOK IS DESIGNED TO WORK WITH IT'S
COMPANION DVDS, ORDER THEM NOW
Little clubs are also available

Watch the web site for tips from the pro on how to improve
and also for advance notice of
appearances and seminars

AND WHILE YOU ARE ON THE WEB SITE
LEAVE AN E-MAIL WITH A TESTIMONIAL OR
A COMMENT ON HOW WE CAN
IMPROVE OUR PRODUCT

Printed in the United States
80596LV00006B/23